FUTURESTORATIVE

WORKING TOWARDS A NEW SUSTAINABILITY

MARTIN BROWN

RIBA ⊞ Publishing

© RIBA Enterprises Ltd, 2016

Published by RIBA Publishing, part of RIBA Enterprises Ltd,
The Old Post Office, St Nicholas Street, Newcastle upon Tyne, NE1 1RH

ISBN 978-1-85946-630-8, 978-1-85946-717-6 (PDF)

The right of Martin Brown to be identified as the Author of this Work
has been asserted in accordance with the Copyright, Designs and
Patents Act 1988 sections 77 and 78.

All rights reserved. No part of this publication may be reproduced,
stored in a retrieval system, or transmitted, in any form or by any
means, electronic, mechanical, photocopying, recording or otherwise,
without prior permission of the copyright owner.

British Library Cataloguing-in-Publication Data
A catalogue record for this book is available from the British Library.

Publisher: Steven Cross
Commissioning editor: Elizabeth Webster
Production: Richard Blackburn
Designed and typeset by Ashley Western
Printed and bound by W&G Baird Ltd in Great Britain
Cover image: Consult Development

While every effort has been made to check the accuracy and quality
of the information given in this publication, neither the Author nor
the Publisher accept any responsibility for the subsequent use of this
information, for any errors or omissions that it may contain, or for any
misunderstandings arising from it.

www.ribaenterprises.com

COVER IMAGE NOTE

The monarch butterfly is considered an important
and iconic pollinator, native to North America with
a multigenerational migration journey that spans
from Mexico to Canada. From a population of more
than 1 billion in the 1990s, there is a grave danger
of extinction within 20 years as the monarch's sole
food source milkweed, is virtually eradicated through
chemicals, and genetically modified agricultural
practices. The monarch butterfly is increasingly
seen as a symbol for hope for a restorative future,
championed, for example, by the David Suzuki
Foundation[1] through their #GotMilkweed campaign.

The classic butterfly effect (the movement of a
butterfly wings triggering storms on the other side
of a continent) has become a metaphor for chaos
theory describing the concept that small, seemingly
insignificant actions can have larger, very significant
consequences. And now the butterfly diagram, central
to circular economy thinking, illustrates the potential
to transform the built environment.

In many ways, the monarch butterfly sums up
FutuREstorative, as a symbol of biodiversity and
fragility but with potential for amazing transformation

[1] http://www.davidsuzuki.org

For Dad (Norris John Brown, 1932–2013),
for passing on his 'make and make do' philosophy
that today would be called circular economy thinking.

For Mike (Mike Wigglesworth, 1958–2015),
for sharing mountains, outdoors and geekery.

THANKS

A thanks to all those who have inspired, encouraged and contributed
to FutuREstorative, including friends and followers across numerous
social media platforms.

Thanks to Elizabeth Webster (RIBA editor) for guidance and support,
Soo and Tom for patience with my endless testing of thoughts, and
Chris for support on research.

CONTENTS

FOREWORD

We are, it is now recognised, living within the Anthropocene age: an age when human activity is a dominant impact on the earth's ecosystems. Our built environment sector is both the cause of and provider of solutions to the climate change problems we face today. Yet, despite great efforts, our sustainability performance indicators are worsening. Moving towards a restorative future is not a luxury but an urgent imperative.

The Living Building Challenge, presenting a pathway to a restorative and Living Future, is still embryonic within the UK. However, through the work of Martin and members of the UK Collaborative – many of whom are included in the impressive list of contributors – it is rapidly gaining traction.

I was delighted to be at the launch of the UK Collaborative back in 2013 and it is hugely encouraging to see the first registered project, to see organisations taking the first steps to register within the ILFI JUST programme and the increasing interest in the ILFI Declare and Living Product Challenge material programmes.

And key to a restorative healthy future, central to **FUTURESTORATIVE** and the Living Building Challenge philosophy, is our relationship with nature, through the understanding and application of approaches such as biophilia, rewilding and biomimicry.

In this book, Martin draws on experience from a career in the built environment, a lifetime of outdoor activity, surfacing concepts from ecology and wildness writers and thinkers alongside today's leading advocates and innovators. There are many examples, concepts and arguments presented here that you will love, like and agree with. Others you will not, and will want to challenge – and that's fine. We need more thinking like **FUTURESTORATIVE** that challenges current and entrenched thinking and, in encouraging debate, moves us forward.

Like the Bullitt Centre, a flagship Living Building Challenge project, our home at the ILFI and a project that has inspired much within this book, **FUTURESTORATIVE** will open doors so that others may follow, apply new thinking to design, build and operate buildings that are truly regenerative, and join us on our journey to a Living Future.

AMANDA STURGEON
FAIA, LEED Fellow
CEO International Living Future Institute

INTRODUCTION
'STAY HUNGRY, STAY FOOLISH'

It is just under three decades since the Brundtland Commission[1] defined Sustainable Development as '*doing nothing today that compromises future generations*'. It was and remains the definitive 'strapline' that has been built into countless sustainability strategies definitions, statements and policies.

We have chosen the '*do nothing*' option, and are compromising future generations.

That may be slightly unfair and it does, of course, depend on who the 'we' is. This book will make and illustrate the case for this Brundtland Commission definition having become, for many, a pretext for allowing the built environment sector to do nothing different, to get away with doing as little as possible, to do just enough to avoid the consequences of noncompliance with legislation, or just to meet client or standard requirements.

The construction sector has been constantly encouraged to rethink with countless improvement and sustainable strategies and directives. Yet many of these strategies have simply washed over the industry with little effect. One of the hardest things to do is learning to let go of the comfortable '*We have always done it this way*' past – yet it is just this that is key to unlocking change. The problem is that this is often only done when facing some sort of impending disaster.

Do we face an impending environmental disaster? Is the built environment culpable? Are we in the built environment playing our part in solutions or still adding to the problem? There is more or less unanimous scientific and increasingly business consensus that we have limited time to correct our course. Increasingly we see climate change consequences through unstable weather events – an example is the UK floods of 2015–16. Indeed it is flooding that will be the most visible and damaging of climate change consequences within the UK.

There are a number of themes running through **FUTURESTORATIVE**.

We do not have the luxury of only being incrementally less bad. We have an amazing array of tools, approaches and practices, with many emerging in the digital arena. We should never be content with using this arsenal to be just a little better, but should make transformational and net-positive improvements across all aspects of our sector.

We have designed, intentionally or not, the construction industry we have: many would say the industry we deserve. We can, and must, redesign the industry and set at its heart a modern sustainability based on nature. Today, unfortunately, whichever sustainability standard we choose, we are still heading towards an irrevocably damaged environment. The 1982 film *Blade Runner* was set in 2019; without change, are we on course to match its dystopian vision of the future environment?

Collaboration is essential, whether through working together or through collaborative development both with those traditionally inside the industry and those who we would see as unconventional partners, e.g. from the health and charity sectors. Sustainability cannot be addressed or solved with a silo mentality.

New sustainability schools of thought and standards for the built environment are emerging, based on ecology, science and health, rather than, or in addition to, finance and business. These new schools of thought – tagged with labels such as deep green, net-positive, restorative and regenerative – are challenging the way we think about sustainability, encouraging us to do different things, and creating a new normal. They represent a vision of true sustainability, one that gives back more than it takes, rather than a merely 'less bad' vision of what we already practice.

About this book

This book is a collection of challenges, innovations and inspirations. The informed narrative and insight from the author, sustainability advocate and consultant Martin Brown, is illustrated with blog-style contributions from UK and international sustainability thought leaders, advocates and practitioners.

Sustainability thinking to date has focused mainly on the design and operation of new buildings. Until recently the author believes its focus on energy efficiency has been blinkered. This book attempts to shift that focus, widening discussion to include the construction process within the new people- and health-based sustainability paradigm.

The aim is to inform and change the conversation, reframe the debate, and advocate for a radical change in direction for built environment sustainability.

Although there is close affinity with the Living Building Challenge, recognised as the built environments most rigorous building performance standard and philosophy, this book is not exclusively based on the Challenge, which represents just one route to approaching restorative or regenerative sustainability. There is no doubt, however, that the Living Building Challenge is just that: a challenge. Some of its imperatives will even be illegal in the UK, and it will certainly test current sustainability thinking right across the built environment. While this journey will not be comfortable, straightforward or easy, it certainly will not be boring, nor based on bureaucratic tick boxes! Without a doubt, such restorative sustainability puts fun and purpose back into sustainable construction.

This, then, is not a book of solutions, of which there are many available, but a book which encourages a different thinking that will enable new solutions for sustainability. It presents a rethinking opportunity for clients, designers, construction, supply, manufacture, facilities management, students and those in academia, as well as sustainability advocates. We all have a hugely important role to play and a hugely important responsibility to collaborate for a restorative and sustainable future.

There are a lot of thoughts and concepts here that take us on a journey from the past, into the present and on to a 'Restorative Future' – a journey from Total Quality Management (TQM) to the circular economy, from ecology to Building Information Management (BIM), from philosophy to fracking, from cycling to living buildings. Throughout, however, the theme is of recognising and addressing the impact and influence of the built environment on our own and our planet's wellbeing.

Central to the **FUTURESTORATIVE** theme is the emergence of a net-positive and restorative sustainability, exploring the shift from the often blinkered focus on sustainability as simply energy performance to a more rounded social, wellness, health and healthy buildings debate. Reconnecting with nature is a theme that weaves throughout the book's narrative. Having lost our real connection with nature we have also lost our respect for it, and are much likelier to tolerate damage done to it.

The influence the built environment has on other sectors is immense. The buildings and facilities we provide and maintain can affect business finance, staff costs, staff health, patient recovery and wellbeing. The built environment strongly affects household finance, pushing or lifting households into or out of fuel poverty. This influence falls soundly within the corporate social responsibility agenda, and raises some thorny questions. For example, is it socially responsible to knowingly design and provide buildings that adversely affect people's health through inclusion of toxic materials?

From the industrial and energy uncertainties of the 1970s to today's digital age, the author has been at the forefront of built environment developments, through project management, business improvement, collaborative working, environmental management, social media and sustainability.

Starting work in the mid 1970s was, looking back, a grim time. It was a time of energy crises of a very different kind than we have now. In December 1973 Edward Heath, then Prime Minister, addressed the nation, with a speech that could, within an energy efficiency context, be relevant today:

....

'As Prime Minister, I want to speak to you, simply and plainly, about the grave emergency now facing our country. In the House of Commons this afternoon I announced more severe restrictions on the use of electricity. You may already have heard the details of these. We are asking you to cut down to the absolute minimum the use of electricity for heating, and for other purposes in your homes.'

....

Thus my work as a junior Quantity Surveyor back in 1973, based on site on a (now demolished) housing project in Bath, was marked by the three-day working week brought in by the government in an attempt to ration energy. Learning to square dims (a QS task that was still in imperial) by gaslight on a freezing cold site office was more akin to something from Dickens than construction in the latter half of the 20th century.

One of my first really exciting projects was a dry dock construction for oil rig assembly on the west coast of Scotland. As a *cost plus* project, the task as Quantity Surveyor was simply to log all project expenditure and add a profit percentage. I now look back with a sense of guilt at the irresponsible approach to resources, expenditure and waste, typical of the construction industry then and, sadly, now. I recently visited the project site, once a symbol for a new age in energy, since converted to a marina and holiday park, and now given new life as a luxury spa and leisure location.

I was at this time listening to west coast rock (The Eagles, Jackson Browne) and I guess, by association, the emerging environmental movement epitomised by the Whole Earth Catalog,[2] made famous in later years by Steve Jobs and others through the movement's '*Stay Hungry, Stay Foolish*' mantra. The phrase describes the need to keep learning with an open mind for change, to question current practice and to explore unconventional approaches, and is as relevant today for sustainability as it was in the 1970s.

Whole Earth Catalog thinking was another way of addressing the energy crisis – through using natural organic building products, sourced locally, and renewable energy. In contrast, the government's agenda fixated on energy security, European and global markets. We missed another opportunity in the 1990s with the UK's coal mine closures – a missed opportunity to invest in emerging renewable energy technologies.

In 1970 the first Earth Day was held in the US, co-organised by Denis Hayes,[3] who I would later meet to discuss the Bullitt Center and the Living Building Challenge in relation to this book.

We all need heroes, and mine have come from the outdoor world as much as anywhere, with Yvon Chouinard[4], environmentalist, mountaineer and founder of the Patagonia company, standing out in particular. The seasonal Patagonia brochures with environmental blog-style editorials and Yvon's profound quotes, such as '*Every time I do the right thing for the environment we make a profit,*' and '*We don't use the word sustainability until we give more back to the environment than we take,*' were an uncomfortable juxtaposition against the sustainability labels we used and continue to use in construction and that we give to projects, products, companies and ourselves.

It was and remains a delight then to discover the Living Building Challenge and to engage with the 2011 ILFI[5] conference via Twitter, and to hear of values and philosophies aligned with outdoor environmentalists and ecologists. Here was a group of people and a school of sustainability that thought the same way I did. It felt like discovering that new music artist you feel you should have heard of many years earlier.

Following visits and meetings in the US and Canada, the UK collaborative was born, launched by Amanda Sturgeon, CEO of ILFI, in 2013. Now, with a handful of passionate ambassadors, we are part of a global network, sharing and advocating a fresh philosophy for the built environment, encouraging certification for UK projects, and delighted to now have a UK-registered project[6] and UK organisations pursuing the related JUST and DECLARE recognition programmes.

When we formed the UK collaborative, it was Mel Starrs,[7] who many will remember fondly as a walking wiki on sustainability standards, who commented that here at last was a standard that could reflect the green aspirations of sustainable organisations. She said: '*If your organisation or projects are aspiring to be green – then this is the sustainability thinking and the standard that you need to aspire to.*'

A Sense of Urgency

In mid 2015, Lord Stern[8], economist and author of the Stern Review on the Economics of Climate Change, warned that current targets and approaches will not be enough to head off climate change and climate disruption. The UNCCC later released data to show that in 2015, the CO_2 concentrate in the atmosphere had risen above 400ppm for the first time in millions of years. And in December 2015, the UK Green Construction Board reported[9] that the target of reducing built environment carbon emissions (by 50% from 1990 levels by 2025) is now out of reach with current practice. We now have a wider gap to bridge than we did in 2009.

Working together, we have to solve this sustainability thing, and urgently – otherwise, as Jason McLennan[10], former CEO of ILFI and founder/architect of the Living Building Challenge, warned in London in October 2015, '*Our children may never see the nature that we saw as children.*'

In Paris in December 2015, something quite remarkable happened. Just under 200 countries agreed to the Paris Agreement to cap global warming at 2°C with an ambition to cap at 1.5°C. For the first time in climate change talks, the impact and influence of buildings and the built environment on climate change was fully recognised.

Unfortunately, our built environment sector has picked up the tag of '*the 40% sector*', an indicative and negative 40% figure for energy use, resource use, waste created, carbon emitted, transport on roads and most likely 40% influence on the nation's health bill.

Author Naomi Klein is correct when she comments that there are no non-radical approaches left before us in addressing climate change.[11] This is something we need to face up to quickly, as the longer we wait, the more radical actions will need to become.

And yet – as Denis Hayes commented in relation to the Bullitt Center and other leading deep-green projects that demonstrate we do have the solutions, the exemplars and the will – once something exists, we can no longer say it is impossible.

Throughout this book we hear of projects, approaches, organisations and people who are passionate not only about reducing this 40% figure but eliminating it – about going beyond net-zero to a net-positive future, one that gives more than it takes.

That is where we all need to be, and fast. We cannot be content to come back in five years' time to talk of a 30% sector. We can and must be better than that.

It is now down to us to take responsibility for that 40% impact and play our role with the necessary advocacy, action and results to turn negative to positive.

At the time of writing, the UK is struggling to comprehend the impact of the June 2016 referendum outcome to leave the EU. The implications of Brexit have been widely recognised as potentially profound and long lasting, with no immediate or clear strategy in place.

In addressing the impacts on a future built environment, (e.g. costs, resources, skills, regulations, trading, education, research), never before have we needed more the mature business and improvement approaches explored within this book and, importantly, a strong restorative sustainability approach.[12]

[1]   Brundtland Commission, Oxford University Press, ISBN 9780192820808
[2]   Whole Earth Catalog: http://www.wholeearth.com/index.php
[3]   Denis Hayes, President of the Bullitt Foundation: http://www.bullitt.org/about/staff/
[4]   Yvon Chouinard: https://en.wikipedia.org/wiki/Yvon_Chouinard
[5]   International Living Future Institute, http://www.living-future.org
[6]   Cuerdon Valley Park Visitor Centre, Preston
[7]   Mel Starrs (1973–2012), http://www.melstarrs.com/elemental
[8]   Lord Stern: http://webarchive.nationalarchives.gov.uk/+/http://www.hm-treasury.gov.uk/independent_reviews/stern_review_economics_climate_change/stern_review_report.cfm
[9]   http://www.constructionmanagermagazine.com/news/construc8tion-2025-emissi4ons-target-slipp5ing/
[10] Jason McLennan: http://www.jasonmclennan.com
[11] Naomi Klein: author, *This Changes Everything*. Quoted at http://thischangeseverything.org
[12] https://fairsnape.com/2016/06/28/brexit-is-moving-uk-from-client-status-into-the-supply-chain/

CHAPTER ONE
THE CHALLENGE

THE PAST

Has anyone else noticed there is an increasing sense of having arrived at some sustainable destination? You might think so, reading client reports and blog posts proclaiming green credentials of that latest project, designers and contractors boasting of innovative sustainable approaches, and with just about every construction material now having some wonderful green credential.

While there is no doubt that we have made great progress, there is danger in thinking of sustainability in any other terms than as a journey. We are only now beginning to understand what sustainability means, only now sorting out route maps and equipment and lacing up our boots for a journey whose destination is as yet uncertain.

Case studies of projects are by and large written just after the construction, so sustainable aspects incorporated describe intent, rather than proven and tested approaches. They are often written as PR material, rather than to inform and progress sustainability. We need far more case studies that show sustainable performance 12 months, 12 years, 120 years into the life of a building, when it has been tested by inhabitants,[1] changed hands a few times, been modified, updated, even up-cycled.

Contractor sustainability claims are arguably slimmer than project case studies – largely based on great policy and strategy intent and having the project management skills to incorporate sustainability technology designed, manufactured and incorporated into the building by other specialists. Where are the case studies highlighting contractors who take the extra step – whether it be innovating with their supply chain off line, developing sustainable approaches to reduce waste, or greening their offices and site accommodation to reflect their values and policies? Far too often contractors will do only what is required by contract, by BREEAM or LEED, and will not do it where it is not required.

OH DEAR: WHAT HAVE WE DONE?

The influence of the built environment on just about every other sector is immense. In addition to its *footprint*, acknowledged as the impact on the environment, we should also really understand its *handprint*, i.e. the positive good we do and the impact we have on those we work with, come into contact with or influence.

In the opening chapter of *Cradle to Cradle: Remaking the Way We Make Things*,[2] Michael Braungart and William McDonough detail an excellent critical parody description of the design criteria for the Industrial Revolution. Similarly no one starting out to design a built environment industry today would include today's negative impacts. Yet somehow along the way we have incorporated and accepted negative impacts as necessary products of the way we do business.

Within the built environment industry, we are experts at creating proposals, presentations, pitches and bids; indeed, for the majority in the sector, it is often the only way to win work. We know what is required by the client, by legislation, by common sense and by those intuitive, unwritten rules or governance for nature and the environment. Yet what we pitch and what we as an industry offer can be very different.

Imagine then, if we were to be brutally truthful and honest in our pitches and bids, we may find ourselves saying:

GOVERNMENT / CLIENT / OWNER

We are aware that our buildings may well become 'sick building syndrome' places, but we need to give priority to cost, programme and availability of materials.

We procure buildings based on the lowest build cost, knowing that running costs, and in particular the energy costs, may escalate. And in the case of domestic property, knowing this will push more people into fuel poverty.

We have created a fragmented sector that now struggles to collaborate and to innovate and hence we accept lowest denominator solutions.

We set up national and regional strategy groups, and develop industry strategies and targets that aim to only make us incrementally less bad.

Concepts of zero and net-positive have been and will continue to be debated, and included in selection criteria – but little will be done to enforce them.

DESIGN

We will continue to be a fossil fuel dependent sector, locking our clients and future-generation users of buildings in to a fossil fuel dependent future.

We struggle with understanding net-positive approaches to design–build.

We are aware that we have designed, built and maintain buildings with poor light and poor air that contribute to poor health, increase staff absenteeism, lower productivity and hence increase running costs for our client's business.

We have designed buildings that discourage users from taking the stairs by placing lifts prominently in the lobby and enticing visitors with shiny 'Ride me' signage.

CONSTRUCTION

We have created millions of tonnes of waste, hidden it in the ground, and will continue to do so where we can. We know that most of it will not decompose but are sure that this problem can be solved by future generations.

We have a culture of low sustainability aspirations, only doing what legislation or the contract demands, rarely doing the right thing for the planet at our expense.

We have created dangerous and harmful work places through construction methods and use of toxic materials.

We create high levels of stress through onerous travel demands on staff.

We employ some of the best project managers and supervisors in the world of construction, and require that they spend their careers in site accommodation with poor daylight and no greenery – yet we build healthy buildings for our clients that foster creativity, health and productivity.

As contractors we invest little in R and D to develop sustainability approaches, relying instead on the requirements of the client to drive sustainability, and develop our skills.

In the interests of lowest build cost we value engineer out sustainability approaches and technologies that have been carefully designed in yet have a high capital cost, even when we know that they bring real life-cycle cost and environment benefit, leading to higher fuel consumption and reduced fitness.

MATERIALS

In the interest of cost and durability we continue using toxic materials even in the face of overwhelming scientific advice, and our own policies of doing 'no harm'. We are aware that our sector has caused lethal illnesses for workers, in the production, installation, removal and treatment of certain materials as waste.

Despite claims of localism focus and of responsible construction, we specify, procure and transport materials around the UK, often based on lowest cost of purchase and availability. Yet we know that 30% of all traffic is construction related, and 70% of a project's carbon footprint is transport related.

KPI HEADLINE PERFORMANCE: DESPITE DECADES OF SUSTAINABILITY AND ENERGY EFFICIENCY RESEARCH AND DEVELOPMENT...

We rarely achieve design performance when the facility is in use. As a sector we have invested much in researching, understanding and attempting to close the Performance Gap.

Carbon emissions of the construction build process have increased.

We struggle to meet waste reduction targets, either in waste generated or waste to landfill.

We do not know the carbon footprint of the UK construction sector.

We do not know the carbon footprint of our organisation.

We are aware that the biggest impact we have on the environment is through travel, yet consider it too difficult to really understand, monitor and reduce.

We do not know the true cost of our organisation, buildings or activities to the ecosystem.

We are not so good at learning and 'closing the loop', but we do try. 'Lessons learnt' exercises are useful... when we have time to do them.

Despite monitoring construction KPIs since Rethinking Construction and environmental KPIs since the built environment sustainability strategies of the 1990s, we rarely close the Deming Cycle loop of Plan, Do, Check, Act. We nearly always get bogged down in the checking, not acting to improve, so each project is planned with the same thinking as the previous one.

OK, so this is a harsh and very much worst-case scenario. Many organisations and projects within the sector demonstrate elements of excellence. Yet there are many elements of truth here too. While the sector has evolved, changed and been shaped by powerful factors (political, economic, legal and technical), we do have an industry largely designed by those within it.

EVERY PROJECT MATTERS

However, while we can see exemplars in large or high-profile projects, it is in the 'long tail' of construction that we are more likely to hear the comments listed above, and where the greatest sustainability impact can occur.

> It really is time to move away from the notion that sustainability is only for big, high-profile projects.

In construction, we regularly hear reasons not to employ sustainability approaches in small projects. These reasons may come from the client ('*We only demand sustainability management on projects over £5m*'), from the contractor ('*We only apply Site Waste Management on projects over £300,000*'), from the subcontractor ('*We only use sustainable timbers on larger projects or when asked*') or from the architect ('*The project is too small to consider BREEAM Very Good*').

THE 'LONG TAIL' OF CONSTRUCTION

Figure 1.1 The term 'long tail', based on statistical distributions, has gained popularity in recent times as a description of the retailing strategy of selling relatively small quantities of a large number of unique items – usually in addition to selling fewer popular items in large quantities. The 'long tail' was popularised by Chris Anderson in an October 2004 *Wired* magazine article.

The 'long tail' of construction helps us understand why every project matters when it comes to sustainability: collectively, the smaller buildings, houses, office and school extensions and beach chalets can have a greater impact than the high-profile, larger projects. This thinking then suggests it is the projects in the 'long tail', not just the higher-value and higher-profile projects, that must have appropriate sustainability standards applied, proportionate to the collective impact.

THE 40% INDUSTRY

Somewhere, somehow, in recent years the built environment sector has picked up the label of being the 40% sector, based on its (mostly) negative impact on the environment. Whilst many of the 40% 'claims' may be seen as anecdotal, even urban myth, they are very close to research based evidence, performance data or published papers.

CONSTRUCTION: THE 40% SECTOR

The built environment generates around 40% of all carbon emissions in the UK.

Construction accounts for 40% of the total flow of raw materials into the global economy every year.[3]

40% of a nation's health costs are attributable to the built environment.

In 2014, 41% of total US energy consumption was consumed in residential/commercial buildings – about 40 quadrillion British thermal units.[4]

Construction consumes over 40% of Europe's energy and resources.

The built environment accounts for 36% of EU CO_2 emissions and 40% of total EU energy.[5]

Lighting represented about 25% of energy use in 2010 and nearly 40% of carbon emissions within the non-domestic sector.

In 2050, capital city carbon will represent nearly 40% of the built environment's emissions (versus 18% in 2010).

40% of construction carbon is locked into material and waste transportation.[6]

Over recent years a number of events and conferences have been held to explore the 40% figure. Perhaps there is even a sense of pride in the 40% tag, rather than a sense of guilt. We should not and cannot be satisfied with targets of reducing carbon by 40% by 2025, for example, or reducing waste to landfill by (just) 50%, as stated in recent strategies.

We need the thinking, courage, leadership and aspiration within the whole industry to turn this around – with aspirations to become the 40% net-positive sector. To consider this impossible is to view impossibility as a fact, not an opportunity or challenge.

HAVE WE WASTED A GOOD CRISIS?

'What's in store for me in the direction I don't take?'

JACK KEROUAC

Never Waste a Good Crisis was a short publication from Constructing Excellence (2009) that focused on collaborative working within a period of recession, developing skills and strengths and importantly relationships, ready for the emergence from the recession into what was anticipated to be – and turned out as – a new era of construction.[7]

During this period of slow activity, we wasted the opportunity to address any maturing of the sustainability agenda. In the 2008–2013 recession, clients, architects and contractors shed staff and saw sustainability as an unnecessary burden and a drain on reducing resources. Now, emerging from that recession, we hear that organisations are just too busy to develop sustainability skills, and that resources remain stretched from the recession's impact.

In a number of workshops and presentations that stretch back to 'business improvement' roles and Total Quality Management days, reference has been made to the very clever 'square wheels' approach from squarewheels.com.[8] In a 2013 blog post, I used the expression 'pedalling squares' to illustrate how progress and development in sustainability is often a clunky and inefficient activity.

Figure 1.2 **New circular improvement tools now available to built environment sustainability.**

There is so much to say about square wheels. The obvious is that we struggle to run our organisations on square wheels and clunky approaches, when the more efficient round wheels are available – we know about them, but they are just not used.

Within construction we have some great new round wheels available to us that will improve our business, our services to clients and our image – for example the tools of BIM, social media and concepts of circular economy and restorative sustainability. These nice new shiny round wheels – carried, or in the store room and not used – are necessary in a construction organisation's baggage. Of course we may take them out and fix them temporarily to the business for PQQ (Pre Qualification Questionnaire), PR and interviews to demonstrate a sense of being tuned into current industry improvement programmes, but then we remove them for business as usual, running once again on square wheels.

SUSTAINABILITY SQUARES[9]

For me, one of the best recent cycling reads has been *Velo* by Paul Fournel,[10] a collection of zen-like thoughts on all things cycling. From one of the brilliant posts, 'Circles': '*To ride a bike is to make circles. You have to think about that when you pedal, as a little reminder the movement of the legs is circular, you have to grant it this and turn the cranks roundly.*' Cyclists have a sense of this. As soon as the cadence falls and fatigue mounts they say they are peddling squares. In fact, cyclists have their own gyroscope, producing not only movement but equilibrium. The faster you turn your legs, the more harmonious this equilibrium becomes.

And so it is with sustainability, or should be: to keep moving forward, we need to keep circling. Think about William Edwards Deming's 'Plan, Do, Check, Act' circle as a means of keeping improvements in equilibrium. The swifter we can progress, the greater the sustainability equilibrium, where all 'competing influences are balanced'. If we slow, become distracted or fatigued, sustainability efforts are no longer circular and become square, cumbersome and energy sapping. And if you stop, you fall off …

LEAN AND SUSTAINABILITY

Construction largely missed out on the Total Quality Management and Benchmarking era of continuous improvement of the 1980s and '90s.

As a TQM and Benchmarking practitioner in the 1990s and 2000s, I heard repeatedly that as the built environment is so different from any other sector, what could it possibly learn from outside the sector? As we shall see throughout this book, there is indeed plenty to learn and adapt from other sectors in the world of sustainability, and the industry may be shifting from 'learning for improvement' to 'learning for survival'.

The built environment dabbled in TQM, enjoying the problem-solving tasks, and quality circles. But TQM never became the strategic improvement priority that it did in other sectors that embraced such approaches and, through learning from other sectors, transformed their own. The legacy of the 1990s improvement era continues as a lone voice in the built environment sector, promoting powerful topics such as lean construction, last planner, even lean BIM, but the use of the classic TQM tools such as Kaizen or Six Sigma to deliver 99% right first time is very much a rare thing in today's construction industry.

Honda ran an advert in 2010 with the catch line '*Everything we do goes into everything we do*'. Unfortunately, taking into account its 30-40% waste and with productivity as low as 60%, the built environment sector is far from making such a claim.

Without the TQM or lean management foundation of other industries, the construction industry is at a disadvantage in moving forward on a number of fronts relating to sustainability. Barriers to improving sustainability include the lack of skilled facilitators and a lack of understanding of root cause analysis.

COST – THE SUSTAINABLE CONSTRUCTION BARRIER

'We have to transition from a distractive economy, to a regenerative one.'

IBRAHIM SALIH - AT LF15 CONFERENCE QUOTED IN TWEET BY ERIC COREY-FREED

We know from the work of Nicholas Stern that the cost of addressing climate change issues will be greater tomorrow than it is today if we don't act now. And so it is within the built environment sector. We know the influence and leverage of buildings on business and occupant expenses, not to mention health, through models such as 1:5:200.

1:5:200

The expression '1:5:200' originated in a Royal Academy of Engineering paper of 1998, 'The Long Term Costs of Owning and Using Buildings',[11] where it was used as a guide to illustrate the cost of ownership of new office buildings. If the capital construction cost is a unit of 1, the facilities management cost will be a factor of 5 and the operating costs a factor of 200, over a 20-year life. 1:5:200 has also been used to illustrate the leverage and impact of sustainability factors across the design, build, facilities management and operating industries within an integrated built environment sector. 1:5:200 has fostered much debate and argument as to its accuracy and usefulness; however the paper's principal message – that concentration on capital cost alone is not providing user or occupant value – is sound.

Ultimately, the economics of green construction and then restorative sustainability will become so compelling that financial change will have to happen. It's how we as an industry prepare for that transition and manage the consequences of change that is important.[12]

From research attached to the Bullitt Center in Seattle (acknowledged by many to be the world's greenest commercial building), we now know that deep-green buildings can pass financial tests and that a *compelling case can be made today that very-high-performance, deep-green buildings can pass financial tests while also delivering a valuable stream of mission-oriented "external" public benefits*.[13]

How then can we make the switch to fully addressing restorative sustainability costs with a project budget? Imagine a world of construction where the lowest common denominator position is for sustainability measures to be *added* into the project through value engineering exercises, rather than at present *removed* through value engineering to meet budgets.

Nudge behaviour theory argues that positive reinforcement and indirect suggestions to try to achieve non-forced compliance can influence the motives, incentives and decision-making of groups and individuals, at least as effectively – if not more effectively – than direct instruction, legislation or enforcement.

Aligned to nudge behaviour is the wonderful Kano 'Delight Theory', which illustrates that what delights us today, and what we will pay more for today, will become an expectation for which we will not pay tomorrow. Examples are seen in the world of white goods and the auto industry, where seat belts, airbags and GPS within cars that once delighted are now expected. And so it has been and will be in buildings regarding health, energy and fitness for purpose. What are considered delights at the moment – whether it be low energy costs through PassivHaus, toxic-free buildings through Living Building Challenge or buildings that foster good health through the WELL Building Standard – will become tomorrow's expectations, and at no additional cost.

But do we really have the luxury of time to nudge? We are starting to understand from models such as the Living Building Challenge what good sustainability means. We have amazing digital BIM-related modelling tools to know what 'good' looks like. We know the cost of good – and we know the real cost of sustainable construction.

However, through the twisted approach of value management and value engineering we reduce 'good' and shoehorn sustainability into project budgets.

Project costs and programmes have become incrementally bloated over recent decades through acceptance of bad, unproductive and wasteful practice. These bad practices include the usual reworking, drawing re-iteration, waste, coordination, poor information flow, communication, attendance, skills and time loss, to name a few – issues that construction project management staff firefight on a daily basis. Having accepted these practices as normal, we seek to include them in the cost of the next project, and they easily become the cost of the way we do things. And in doing so we divert cost away from achieving the 'good' originally envisioned.

The Bullitt Center's original vision of a fossil-fuel-free building was held firmly by Denis Hayes, who repeatedly turned down design proposals that included fossil fuel options. Such commitment, patience and rigidity from Hayes resulted in design and construction teams innovating to realise his vision. The Bullitt Center would have been a very different building had design teams concluded it was impossible and not sought alternatives, or had the project team compromised and shoehorned their vision into lower budgets.

The next generation deepest green buildings must extend this commitment, patience and vision to the construction phase. They must not accept value engineering that reduces value, not accept waste as an option, not accept the use of fossil fuel in construction. Innovation will only develop from strict standards which prohibit unsustainable practices.

Imagine if we could deliver net-positive sustainable projects that are less costly.

Building on previous industry collaborative cost development thinking, we can deliver improved value and 'good' at the right price. But we must urgently re-examine and eliminate the Muda costs associated with construction. (Muda is the brilliant Japanese term encompassing all kinds of waste, from quality issues to material waste, wasted time, energy, water and more.) In fact we need to go further than eliminating, and move into a restorative sustainability thinking mode where, for example, we are not focusing on reducing waste, but on constructing with less material.

If, as research and data is showing (see page 20), Muda in construction can be in the region of 30-40% or more, it is essential to attack this element through lean thinking. Then, rather than 'reducing 'good' to fit current wasteful practices', we can afford 'good' at a lower cost, or potentially reclaim that wasted 30–40% to afford 'good'.

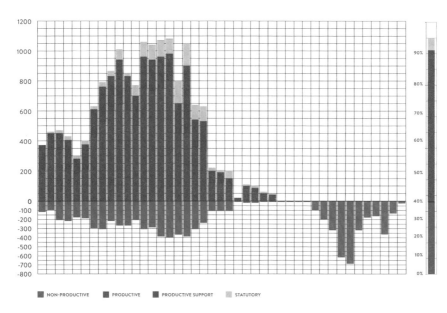

Figure 1.3 Construction: 37% unproductive. Source: IBE Partnerships

POOR LEADERSHIP IS THE ROOT CAUSE OF CONSTRUCTION MUDA

Drilling down, asking (more than) the Five Whys, we can come to understand the root cause of Muda.

Figure 1.4 Poor Leadership is the root cause of construction Muda. Source IBE Partnerships

Reducing Waste, then, should be the construction industry's biggest contribution to the sustainability agenda, and a key aspect that should be included in sustainability processes and standards. If responsible construction is about providing sustainability, then restricting or preventing sustainability through wasteful, unproductive costs is irresponsible, and something we in the construction sector should be ashamed of.

Alongside the brutally honest pitches that opened this chapter, what if we were honestly accountable to building users? *'We're sorry you didn't get the sustainable, deep-green building you envisioned and that your fuel costs will remain high, but our wasteful processes and practices distracted too much from the project costs.'*

Unfortunately it is the prevalent lowest-cost procurement mindset that presents one of the biggest barriers to green building. Current accounting and costing practices are compromising future generations, preventing future building users and occupants from achieving the necessary green lifestyles and, at worst, keeping many in fuel poverty.

THE CHALLENGE – A RESTORATIVE SUSTAINABILITY COST MODEL FOR CONSTRUCTION

From Alfred Bossom through Building Down Barriers, Constructing Excellence to Construction 2025 we have nearly 100 years of research, evidence, industry thinking and strategy to reduce costs and add value.[14] Yet the cost-value relationship remains poorly understood, particularly when it comes to adding sustainability value.

Let's look at a simplified model of arriving at a construction price, and a model for pricing restorative sustainability:

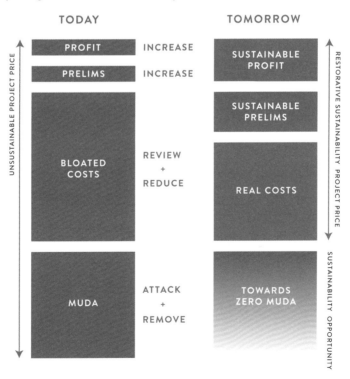

Figure 1.5 A restorative sustainability cost model: the construction price of a project

Current Approach – The 'Old Way'

■ Profit – competitive: **Most often determined through competition, and reduced to the lowest possible to win work. Low profit for the contractor and hence the supply chain at best inhibits sustainability. Increased profit enables sustainable growth and development, staff training and innovation, and social responsibility.**

■ Overheads – competitive: **Again, determined most often through competition to the lowest possible overheads in order to win work. Low overheads and prelims inhibit sustainable management on projects, whereas improved correct-level margins enable more sustainability resources, such as a sustainability facilitator, green accommodation, green travel and more.**

■ Competitive costs – The labour plant and material costs: **developed uncollaboratively, in competition, which results in lowest cost and inhibits sustainability. Not reflective of the real cost of doing the work, as bids are often bloated by including unproductive practices carried from one project to the next.**

■ Muda – *'Everything we do that doesn't go into what we do'*: **The time, effort, material, waste and energy used on the project and which do not contribute to the final building. The 2005 time and motion study undertaken and illustrated in Figure 1.3 shows time wasted on projects can be 37%. Reducing the Muda to zero through lean construction approaches should be the objective of every project; to call this impossible is only a mindset. Releasing Muda costs will generate the levels of profit and margin that will enable sustainable construction.**

And note that Muda is the zone that gives the most worry, whether it's stress from firefighting at site level or boardroom angst when projects go wrong. If we are concerned with addressing the image of construction and reducing stress levels on site, this is the key area to attack.

A New Approach – A Restorative Sustainability Cost Model

- Sustainable profits – **Fixed, agreed, what the organisation needs to develop sustainability, to invest in training, research and development**

- Sustainable margins – **The correct level of margins for the project, ensuring correct sustainability infrastructure, accommodation, facilitation, training, continuous improvement**

- Sustainable costs – **The real costs–the lean costs–of doing the task(s) with no historic unproductive element**

- Sustainability opportunity costs – **The balance, derived from any remaining Muda. Ideally targeted at 100% of the original Muda cost.**

WHERE ARE WE? ... FROM GREY TO BRIGHT GREEN

We all approach sustainability from different perspectives, and with differing senses of responsibility. To understand these perspectives and their impact, the author has used the Fairsnape 'Grey to Bright Green' exercise in workshops and consultation as a starter for discussions on sustainability strategy over the last decade.[15] It asks questions about where we really are, where we should be, and where our staff, our clients, the next generation or our children think we are.

GREY TO BRIGHT GREEN

GREY

QUESTIONING
Do nothing today, technology and others will solve our problems tomorrow.

QUESTIONS
CLIMATE CHANGE

FAUX GREEN

ACCOMMODATING
Do the minimum possible, led by legislation, regulation and client requirements.

SEES SUSTAINABILITY
AS A COSTLY CHORE

GREEN

BENEFITING
Realising opportunities and benefits from green approaches.

INVESTS IN
THE FUTURE

BRIGHT GREEN

RESTORING
Doing more good, not just less bad, with net-positive thinking.

HEALS
THE FUTURE

Figure 1.6 Grey to bright green

Grey: A cornucopian perspective, one that questions climate change and the need for sustainability, the cup of sustainability will continue to refresh itself. There is no need to change approaches today as some innovation or new technology will come along tomorrow and make everything OK. It's easy to understand this approach given the daily promises of technology that will solve our problems, such as carbon capture schemes, meaning we can continue as before, using fossil fuels.

Increasingly we see fewer and fewer people or organisations voting for this position, but there are still strong voices advocating that we need do nothing today.

Perhaps a current construction misapprehension is waste to energy. After years of effort to achieve KPIs in diverting waste from landfill through site waste management plans, segregation on site and other approaches, we can now ship everything to a waste-to-energy plant, knowing we will have 100% diverted from landfill on the waste reports. We can then proudly report this to clients and frameworks, include the figure in PQQs and display it on site office walls.

The grey end of the spectrum also includes those who may not be deniers but just don't see the point in making any effort to address sustainability or environmental matters. Those at this end of the spectrum can tend to sap energy from those they work with, preventing them from progressing with their own sustainability goals.

Faux green – An accommodationist perspective. Until recently the more common, and in some groups the only perspective on sustainability. It is one that seeks only to accommodate the minimum required, to accommodate legislation or contractual requirements, with little or no change to the way they do business.

Whenever this exercise has been held within the built environment groups, most delegates recognised themselves or their organisations as having an accommodationist perspective, driven by legislation, contractual or standard requirements. We are legal, runs the thinking, and we met client requirements; why should we do more?

A key aspect to this pattern of thinking is where sustainability and corporate social responsibility (CSR) sit within any organisation. If, for convenience, they sit alongside Health and Safety functions, they may always remain a bolt-on, making it difficult for sustainability to take on a role with a strong voice at board level.

Not surprisingly, those who see themselves as accommodationists also see environmental and sustainability activity as a burden, a costly chore that yields little or no return on investment. In fact there is often little investment over and above that required, with development issues on the project often addressed with client or project money.

Green – A benefiting perspective. Thinking is based on the premise that sustainability makes good business sense, moving beyond the minimum and starting to embed CSR within the organisation. CSR and sustainability, as functions, sit at the centre of the organisation; there is often a dedicated CSR post with a voice at board level. Business impact understanding goes beyond the environmental and includes assessments on, for example, diversity or equality impact.

Encouragingly we now see more companies in this category. They see the benefit of investment in sustainability, whether that's in people or resource investment. The benefits may be business related, in terms of winning work, or improving the organisation's green image.

Bright green – A restorative thinking perspective, stemming from a realisation of a greater holistic good as the driver for sustainability approaches, alongside a recognition of connection with nature or the planet. This is the camp of the net-positive thinkers, those that understand ecology-founded, restorative sustainability, and those who, aware of the wider benefit to nature, the environment, communities and society, seek payback beyond that which returns to the organisation. Often passionate advocates, who inspire and zap energy to (rather than sap energy from) those with whom they work.

TIME TO MOVE ON, THE PAST IS ANOTHER WORLD ...

We can and must reignite sustainability, set the sustainability soul on fire, make sustainability fun and exciting, and inspire a new generation – not only for a vision of sustainability that is regenerative but a vision that also acknowledges the damage of the past and makes amends, healing the future.

A World of Solutions

Within the built environment we may never face an ecological challenge as big as we do today, and without intervention the challenge will likely only grow in difficulty and cost. As Jason McLennan pointed out in his first UK keynote speech (London, October 2015), urgency is required: '*We have to address all problems, for the one we don't address will be our undoing.*'

Fortunately, we have accessible new tools, fresh approaches and inspiring thinking at our disposal, easing the transition to a new age.

We are in the process of rethinking sustainability leadership, rethinking education, rethinking built environment design, rethinking construction process for an ecological age. And importantly we are rethinking buildings and structures as healthy, living entities: as living buildings.

Improving the image of construction is high on the agenda at the moment on many levels, from reputation to career attractiveness and construction visual image. We can remove the stress, the problems, the waste, and lift ourselves from a downward spiral of problems to an industry where every act of construction makes the world a better place. It is not impossible. It is happening already, in many deep-green projects around the world. And as Denis Hayes, Bullitt Center Foundation and Earth Day co-founder stated in a 2015 interview as part of the Sustainability Leadership Conversation series, *'Once something exists we can no longer say it's impossible.'*[16] Impossible is just a challenge, and we relish challenges in construction.

To paraphrase the philosopher Martin Heidegger, *'To build a new vision of the world, we need to understand what it means to live in it.'*[17] The following chapters set out inspirations and challenges, case studies, possible routes and approaches for moving on from the past, enabling us to start designing, constructing and living for the built environment sector we want. And in which every single act will matter.

---

[1]   Inhabitants – an emerging term for occupants in deep-green buildings who inhabit a designed and constructed eco-system

[2]   Braungart, M., and W. McDonough, *Cradle to Cradle: Remaking the Way We Make Things*, New York, North Point Press, 2002.

[3]   http://www.businessandbiodiversity.org/construction.html

[4]   http://www.eia.gov/tools/faqs/faq.cfm?id=86&t=1

[5]   https://ec.europa.eu/energy/en/topics/energy-efficiency/buildings

[6]   www.constructco2.com

[7]   http://constructingexcellence.org.uk/resources/never-waste-a-good-crisis

[8]   http://fairsnape.com/2013/12/04/are-you-running-on-square-wheels

[9]   http://fairsnape.com/2013/08/14/sustainability-in-equilibrium-or-pedalling-squares

[10]   Velo, P. F., ISBN 978-0-9568624-1-9, Roulier Ltd, 2012.

[11]   Evans, R. et al., 'The Long Term Costs of Owning and Using Buildings', Royal Academy of Engineering, 1998.

[12]   http://www.triplepundit.com/2015/09/250-trillion-green-economic-revolution

[13]   From Bullit Center Financial Case Study: http://www.bullittcenter.org/2015/04/02/bullitt-center-financial-case-study/

[14]   Bossom, A. Building to the Skies: The Romance of the Skyscraper (1934)

[15]   www.Fairsnape.com/about

[16]   Insights from a Sustainability Leadership Conversation with Denis Hayes https://fairsnape.com/2014/08/05/restorative-sustainability-once-something-exists-no-one-can-say-its-impossible

[17]   http://www.iep.utm.edu/heidegge/

CHAPTER TWO
FUTURESTORATIVE
KEY CONCEPTS

...at a single thing in nature, he finds it attached to the rest of the world - John Muir 1838 - 1914

KEY CONCEPTS

There are a number of concepts that run throughout this book, forming a foundation for rethinking the way we can approach the design, building and operation of buildings, the way we manage organisations, and the sustainability culture within the built environment sector, to progress towards a restorative future. These key concepts are introduced here as a primer and further illustrated later in the book.[1]

CHANGE – THE TIPPING POINT

> We are in transition phase, with tipping points possible and occurring in any number of sustainability areas.

The 'tipping point' forms an essential element within complexity and chaos theory thinking. Popularised by Malcolm Gladwell's book *The Tipping Point*,[2] the term describes the way systems can absorb influences with minimal change until a 'tipping point' is reached, when there is a sudden and dramatic change.

Currently the built environment sustainability agenda is absorbing a lot of pressure to change. This thinking is present throughout this book to illustrate transition and tipping points. This then results in a sudden shift to a new set of norms and new ways of doing things.

Management guru Charles Handy's sigmoid curve thinking illustrates how a market moves from one state to another through transition and tipping points.[3] This model is adapted throughout this book to illustrate transition and tipping points, from current norms (sustainability business as usual) to new norms (restorative sustainability thinking).

However, cause and effect is not always predictable. Small amounts of input may have large output effects (the SILO effect – '*small in large out*'), while substantial variations on the input side may have minimal effect in altering a system. The now well-known 'butterfly effect' illustrates a situation where small changes in an initial condition can have major and unpredictable consequences elsewhere.

In addition, sustainable construction could be understood as a 'complex adaptive system', where self-organising systems have a capacity to learn and adapt from experience, based on simple rules. The flocking pattern of birds may seem complex, but computer simulation show three simple rules at play: to keep going, to keep the same distance and aim to move to centre of the flock.

Of note here, too, is the trim tab – the small trim rudder, used to change the direction of the main rudder and hence alter the direction of an ocean liner, given the right initial conditions of sea, wind and environment.[4]

Given the right 'initial conditions', tipping points in built environment sustainability will occur, from the emerging pressure of small changes (analogous to the way the trim tab rudder works), alongside advocacy that challenges current sustainability norms.

WE ARE NATURE

'Instead of waiting for some miraculous, high-tech solution to bail us out of our climate-change disaster, the real miracle turns out to be simply working with nature instead of against it.'

YVON CHOUINARD

A common thread in the writings and work of ecologists and environmentalists is the recognition that we are part of nature, not apart from nature, and that we need to work with nature, not against it.

'*We abuse the land because we regard it as a commodity belonging to us. When we see the land as a community to which we belong we may begin to use it with love and respect.*' These words could have been written by current day ecologists, or could well be an extract from the Living Building Challenge's *Place* handbook. In fact, they were written nearly 70 years ago by Aldo Leopold in *A Sand County Almanac*, a widely acknowledged diary that provided a touchstone for ecology and environmentalist thinking.[5] Leopold's philosophies and words reflect the works of earlier environmentalist writers, such as Henry David Thoreau's *Walden*[6], and would be further echoed in Rachel Carson's *Silent Spring*,[7] E.O. Wilson's *Biophilia*[8] and, today, George Monbiot's *Feral*[9] or the work of environmental activist David Suzuki, who notes: '*You can't shoehorn nature into human agendas.*'[10]

While there has always been an ecologist thinking fraternity within the built environment sustainability agenda, ecology thinking has unfortunately remained on the fringes of mainstream construction. Now, though, it is emerging as central to a new era of standards, those with an ecological philosophy as foundation.

How we understand and recognise our relationship with nature is reflected in our approach to sustainability. As the degree of this relationship weakens, so does our respect for nature and consequently our tolerance for doing harm.

REGENERATIVE HEALTH

Sick building syndrome is, sadly, a legacy of the construction industry, yet we are now seeing a welcome recognition of the influence of buildings on health. '*Health is the New Green*' is an increasingly common headline in blogs, sustainability, design and construction journal articles. However we can and must move further, to flip our approach from an industry that is satisfied with delivering *fewer* sick buildings to one that delivers *net-positive* health, where buildings improve health.

The wider healthy settings agenda is also influencing this flip in thinking, embracing ideas of **salutogenesis**, a term coined by Aaron Antonovsky that literally means '*generation of health*'.[11] The word describes an approach which focuses on factors supporting human health and well-being, rather than on factors that cause disease.

The impact on health of design, construction quality and building products is gaining recognition through current wellness agendas. Adoption of **the precautionary principle** is considered key to progressing with healthy materials and eliminating toxic materials from buildings. The precautionary principle states that if an approach or product has any suspected risk of causing human or environmental harm, then, in the absence of scientific consensus that the approach or product is harmful, the burden of proof that it is not harmful falls on those undertaking the design, specifying or procuring products.

Net-positive health or salutogenic buildings that follow the precautionary principle are achievable, given an appropriate mindset, and should be a core objective within any responsible modern built environment sustainability strategy.

RESOURCING WITHIN PLANETARY BOUNDARIES

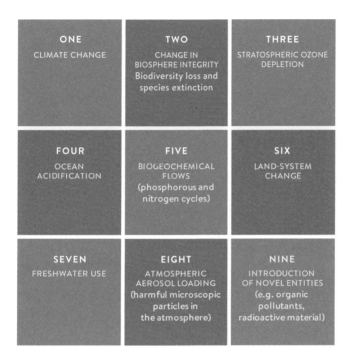

Figure 2.1 The nine planetary boundaries

We must resource from within boundaries that the planet can support.

First introduced in 2009, the framework concept of planetary boundaries defines a set of nine parameters within which we can continue to develop and thrive for generations to come.[12] Crossing these boundaries could generate abrupt and/or irreversible environmental changes.

Early in 2015, researchers writing in the journal *Science* identified that four of the nine planetary boundaries have now been crossed as a result of human activity: climate change, loss of biosphere integrity, land-system change and altered biogeochemical cycles (phosphorus and nitrogen).

The built environment influences and impacts upon all nine planetary boundaries. At present the impact is negative, roughly calculated at a 40% negative. However, through adopting restorative sustainability approaches, the built environment sector can exert a positive impact and edge us back from the boundaries.

The built environment is a huge user of resources. New thinking and approaches, such as net-positive waste, circular economy and cradle to cradle, will allow us to better understand and operate within planetary boundaries.

INFLUENTIAL RESPONSIBILITY

The influence of the built environment ripples into just about every industrial, commercial and domestic sector, in turn influencing these sectors' capability for organisational or lifestyle sustainability. We need to understand that influence and act with due responsibility through sound governance.

Governance is the term that describes how internal rules, norms and actions are developed, sustained, regulated and held accountable. Eco-governance shapes an organisation's sustainability, ecological and responsibility culture, as well as its members' values and passion for a sustainable future.

In 2015 the UN published its Sustainability Development Goals 2030.[13] The SDGs define the intention to change the Brundtland definition of sustainability from '*Do nothing today that compromises tomorrow's generation*' to a new purpose that is proactive and net-positive, and one that improves the social, environment and financial wellbeing of people and the planet by 2030. Just as we embraced the Brundtland definition, so we must now embrace the SDGs as a foundation for our sustainability visions and strategies.

Understanding and addressing the huge influence of the built environment is essential. It must be included as an organisational governance issue which enables a culture of restorative approaches and delivery.

RETHINKING FOR A RESTORATIVE FUTURE

Learning from those who have gone before us, and setting our new direction of travel.

The term 'rethinking' is one with which the construction industry is familiar, if not always comfortable. It is a legacy of the Sir John Egan Rethinking Construction report, published in 1998, which became the touchstone for all improvement for a generation.[14] Sadly, that report lacked any environmental and sustainability thinking. Now, then, is the time to rethink construction once again, and to understand what value the industry provides today, given that the value mix now includes community, social and environmental elements – for example the thorny financial issues relating to the cost of nature and cost of carbon.

In addition, we have a whole arsenal of thinking, writings and case studies, both from within the architectural and built environment sector and from the world of ecology, sustainability and environmentalism, to help us rekindle and reimagine the future.

Using an expression from Google (derived from John F. Kennedy's *We go to the Moon*' speech of 1966), there is a need to 'Moonshot' construction. A moonshot is an ambitious and groundbreaking exploration for future scenarios. Google uses the expression for a) addressing huge problems, and b) proposing radical solutions, developing breakthrough technology. Rather than incremental improvements in industry strategies, construction moonshots would leapfrog us from where we are to where we need to be, and then 'backcast' a route to get us there. (Backcasting is a methodology, important within sustainability development, that envisions a desirable future scenario and then develops plans, strategies and policies to reach that vision.)

We need that new vision and narrative for sustainability. As leaders, teachers, consultants, practitioners, constructors and operators we can and must rethink and develop a new, shared understanding of sustainability, with new stories, a new language and new thinking.

COLLABORATION – A NEW COLLECTIVE POWER

'We believe that the innovations required to create the future won't come from a single source. Not from science. Not from technology. Not from governments. Not from business. But from all of us. We must harness the collective power of unconventional partnerships to dramatically redefine the way we thrive in the future.'

HANNAH JONES, GLOBAL HEAD OF SUSTAINABILITY AND INNOVATION, NIKE

Our built environment collaborative working journey is now venturing into new territories. The future for a responsible built environment involves increasing pressures and opportunities for thinking and acting differently. This will require moving beyond 'business as usual' collaboration and partnership to co-create, working in hybrid projects, moving to open innovations that in turn stimulate further opportunities.

Our collaborative capacity will be tested by the new and emerging agendas for the sector, including social responsibility, managing increasingly scarce resources in purpose-driven circular economies, addressing restorative sustainability, and adopting transparency while meeting the challenges of BIM and social media transparency.

Decades of strategies have urged built environment improvement through collaborative working. Those organisations that have embraced collaboration have emerged as the stronger and more successful, whereas those who retain uncollaborative approaches – or who revert 'to type' during hard times – have disappeared or continue to struggle.

Collaboration is key to delivering restorative sustainability.

1   More background content can be found through the bibliography within Chapter 8
2   Gladwell, M., *The Tipping Point*, ISBN 0-316-31696-2, 2000.
3   Handy, C., *The Empty Raincoat*, ISBN: 0099301253, 1995.
4   *Trim Tab* is also the inspired name of the International Living Future Institute journal: http://living-future.org/ilfi/trim-tab-blog/trim-tab-magazine
5   Leopold, A., *A Sand County Almanac*, ISBN: 9780195007770, 1949.
6   Thoreau, H.D., *Walden*, ISBN 9781505297720, 1854.
7   Carson, R., *Silent Spring*, ISBN: 2907532742188, 1962.
8   Wilson, E.O., *Biophilia*, Harvard University Press, ISBN 9780674074422, 1984.
9   Monbiot, G., *Feral*, ISBN 9780226205694, 2014.
10 David Suzuki, http://www.davidsuzuki.org (quote from Guardian interview: http://www.theguardian.com/australia-news/2015/sep/24/environmental-activist-david-suzuki-on-tony-abbott-solar-panels-and-his-book)
11 For more information on the salutogenic model, see http://heapro.oxfordjournals.org/content/11/1/11.abstract
12 Planetary Boundaries: Stockholm Resilience Centre http://www.stockholmresilience.org
13 Sustainability Development Goals 2030, United Nations, http://www.un.org/sustainabledevelopment/sustainable-development-goals
14 Egan Rethinking Construction, HMSO, 1998, http://constructingexcellence.org.uk/wp-content/uploads/2014/10/rethinking_construction_report.pdf

CHAPTER THREE
HEALING THE FUTURE

'Impossible is not a fact,
it is an attitude.' CHRISTIANA FIGUERES[1]

OUR COMMON HOME

> 'Given the interrelationship between living space and human
> behaviour, those who design buildings, neighbourhoods, public
> spaces and cities ought to draw on the various disciplines which
> help us to understand people's thought processes, symbolic
> language and ways of acting.'

POPE FRANCIS[2]

This chapter explores a number of approaches that will challenge but also inspire
new thinking. The approaches covered here would have been termed 'soft' in more
traditional management terminology – yet there is nothing soft or easy about changing
established mindsets. Without a shift in thinking, the innovative 'hard' technology
approaches necessary to address climate change, will remain just that: innovative ideas
that are not embraced or embedded into everyday design, construction and operation
of buildings.

Connected with Nature

> 'Wilderness is not a luxury but a necessity of the human spirit.'

EDWARD ABBEY

We cycled slowly, climbing up the steep hill out of the port as dusk fell. A few minutes
earlier, the ferry that had slid through a mirror sea was illuminated below us in the
port. As we approached the breast of the hill, the full moon became visible over the
mountains of Jura. No words were necessary; it was an achingly beautiful moment.
The steepness of the hill disappeared; we stopped, we stared in awe.

We have all had these moments when something triggers a connection with the natural
world. We feel good, not knowing why, but are happy to absorb and breathe deep the
moment. When we remember a favourite place, or recall moments where we have felt
content, we are most likely picturing a place out of doors, surrounded by nature, trees
or landscapes. Unfortunately, such moments are not that common, and becoming

increasingly scarce as we grow accustomed to spending more time indoors, in buildings that isolate us from the outdoors. Yet it is our powerful, intrinsic, yet poorly understood connection with nature that is core to the concept of biophilia.

We rarely get this connection with spaces that we occupy on a regular basis: our home, our office or our workplace. What, then, can we do to employ this connection in these spaces? How can we increase our sense of feeling good, of wellbeing? How can we maintain health and possibly increase productivity, in what we want to achieve socially, domestically or workwise?

In a recent revision to the *Oxford Junior Dictionary* a number of entries no longer deemed appropriate to were deleted and replaced by more modern entries. As nature writer Robert Macfarlane noted: '*The deletions included acorn, adder, ash, beech, bluebell, buttercup, catkin, conker, cowslip, cygnet, dandelion, fern, hazel, heather, heron, ivy, kingfisher, lark, mistletoe, nectar, newt, otter, pasture and willow.*' These were replaced by block-graph, blog, broadband, bullet-point, celebrity, chatroom, committee, cut-and-paste, MP3 player and voice-mail. As Macfarlane said: '*For "blackberry", read "Blackberry"*'[3]. This emphasises the need to re-wild our language as a precursor to understanding the importance of connectivity.

Rachel Carson, author of *Silent Spring* – the 1962 book that, by focusing on the health issues arising from toxic chemicals, in many ways launched the environmental movement – noted, '*The more clearly we focus our attention on the wonders and realities of the universe about us, the less taste we shall have for destruction.*'

Over 50 years later, as we continue to weaken our connection with nature and, through the built environment, become increasingly isolated from nature, we are in turn losing respect for it. Doing so increases our tolerance for causing harm and damage. This, unfortunately, is reflected in our sustainability thinking and the decisions we make for building designs, construction and in-use management.

Over the years one of the author's consultancy and workshop activities has been 'Benchmarkwalks'. These walks, held in numerous country parks (in Bowland Fells and the Lake District) emerged from the 1990s/2000s established benchmarking practice of site visits. 'Benchmarkwalks' sought to provide an alternative to the often stuffy and restrictive sharing and learning that was taking place within factory, hotel or office rooms up and down the country. It soon became apparent that the level of discussion and learning on these walks was more focused than the meeting room versions, encompassing social, business and technical knowledge sharing.

'Benchmarkwalks' was devised with the aim of doing something different, introducing an element of fun into benchmarking. However, research is showing that exposure to nature benefits us in so many ways, and has profound implications for sustainability within the built environment at design, construction and maintenance levels – but also at strategy, sustainability and organisational governance levels.

Research shows that there are different outcomes between groups exposed to natural environments and those exposed to built environments.[4] Research from John Zelenski and others at Carleton University in Ottawa has explored the link between experiencing the natural world and behaving in a sustainable way.[5] The findings support the fact that decisions made when exposed to nature are more sustainable, more cooperative and more socially responsible compared to those made when exposed only to built environment surroundings.

The environment in which we shape and deploy our thinking now leads us towards a future that is more connected to a relationship with technology at the expense of the environment, rather than towards a sustainability relationship with nature supported by technological thinking. It is not surprising that sustainability is often seen not as a benefit, but as a burden that hampers progress and profit.

HOW WE MAY BE SHAPING THE UNSATISFACTORY SUSTAINABILITY OF OUR BUILDINGS:	
Governance and policy	Strategies, policies and rules that shape our industry and organisations are developed in boardrooms or hotel conference rooms.
Education	We are attempting to educate, inspire and prepare future generations within classrooms devoid of natural light, views and 'green' elements.
Development	Sustainability workshops and training sessions are held in training rooms in artificial light or in the same hotel conference rooms as strategy was developed.
Building design	Designs are shaped and developed in soulless cubicle design 'factories'.
Construction	Construction is managed by project teams working in dirt-grey cabins, interiors of partially completed buildings or basements lacking any natural light or views.
Operation	Facilities management and maintenance is carried out by teams housed in the building's service areas and basements.

The Bhutan measure of Gross National Happiness[6] is a key measure of national prosperity, and as Dr Marcia Rocha, (Head of Climate Policy Team at Climate Analytics) commented on a 2015 visit, she saw a country culturally very connected to nature, one where nature is an important focus of their politics.[7] The GNH index is founded on the concept of wellbeing (spiritual, physical and environmental health of the population) and is often considered a better measure than the more traditional finance-related GDP. It seems remarkable that many years after Bhutan introduced their wellbeing measure (initially a topic for mockery), corporate organisations are now developing measures and KPIs of a similar nature.

After all, the wellbeing of an organisation's people is key to how the internal culture will flourish, how the organisation will address sustainability and social responsibility issues, whether the organisation will sap energy from or zap energy to those it works and collaborates with.

HEALTH – A NEW PERFORMANCE GAP

We are increasingly hearing in sustainability circles, corporate social responsibility (CSR) events, journals and blogs that '*health is the new green*' – and rightly so. As we will explore in Chapter 6, new sustainable building certification standards are moving to address the wellbeing, comfort and health of occupants. This is no surprise given staff-related costs for many organisations outweigh energy costs, so keeping staff healthy, inspired, creative and productive through healthy buildings is, alongside energy performance, a key driver. Added to this, we spend 90% of our time inside buildings. Healthy buildings should become a no-brainer.

It has been estimated that buildings can affect or account for 40% of health costs, again illustrating the influence the built environment has on lifestyle and health. Yet although we are now designing healthy buildings we are perhaps still in the 'less bad' trap rather than the 'more good' paradigm. We focus on preventing people getting poorly and on what makes people ill, rather than adopting a salutogenic approach focusing on what can make people better and healthier.

There are examples of projects that set out with the intention of improving health – for example birth centres designed to improve the birth experience, such as at the Dyson Centre for Neonatal Care at RUH Bath,[8] and the collaborative research work in the US (Ariadne Labs and MASS Design) which looks at the impact of birth centre and labour suite design on clinical decision-making in respect of the high caesarean birth rates.[9]

While writing this, an article in the *Guardian* raised the question of whether energy efficient buildings make people sick.[10] There is nothing new in this misperception in the press; in the summer of 2013, according to the *Daily Mail*, 'Green Deal' energy efficient homes were killing residents through overheating.[11] Energy efficiency advocates are quick to point out that it is poor ventilation, often coupled with poor construction quality and the inclusion of toxic materials that off-gas in unventilated spaces, that causes ill health – not PassivHaus, Green Deal or other sustainability principles themselves.

We perhaps should not be surprised at such reports. By designing to maximise energy efficiency and reduction, and not for holistic comfort, we fail to address factors such as ventilation, air quality and natural lighting, meaning we are in danger of creating additional health problems. As Elrond Burrell points out in Chapter 6, PassivHaus is really about comfort.

Rarely if ever do we design to *improve* occupant health in the same way we design to *reduce* energy consumption. We can and should be designing for net-positive health and energy. The two are not incompatible; we simply need to adjust focus.

And that focus is starting to shift with the news that the NHS is to collaborate with clinicians, designers and technology advisors on new healthy towns across the UK, with healthy homes where the obesogenic environment is 'designed out' and health and wellbeing 'designed in'.[12]

Historically, the building performance gap refers to the difference between design predictions and actual performance in relation to energy (and occasionally air quality). Today a new performance gap is emerging: that between health design prediction and the actual impact on occupant health.

'*Simple concepts like comfort, joy and aesthetics have had no place in traditional hospitals,*' notes Jan Golembiewski in her article 'Salutogenic design – The neural basis for health promoting environments', 'yet they are the psychological bricks and mortar of all healthy buildings whether or not they are health care buildings.' [13]

In the same way that we now often monitor and display, in real time, the water energy and air-quality performance of a building, the public health sector has made perhaps even more impressive advances in monitoring health issues such as asthma and diabetes in real time. It is a logical development to link smart building performance monitoring with smart health monitoring devices. By doing so, we add a new dimension to the building performance gap: the building's negative or positive impact on occupant health.

Imagine the synergy of smart building performance data combined with real time health data, embedded within a BIM system, that can be used not only for future design but for real time, net-positive health interventions.

This raises many questions, however. How far do we want to venture down the technology route for real time health interventions? Yes, we need data on how buildings affect the health of inhabitants, so that we can improve them – but that needs to be matched with human intervention, a mindfulness approach that combines the skills of occupational health, facilities management and organisational management.

Stress levels within the construction industry are perhaps among the highest of all industry. It is encouraging to note that the Considerate Constructor Scheme recently focused on mental health awareness, raising the issue at site level, increasing awareness through posters, and encouraging the training of first aiders in dealing with mental health. Unfortunately, at the time of writing, it hasn't yet increased awareness or addressed the *root causes* of poor mental health in the construction industry.

Early in my career, when I was cutting teeth on construction sites in the 1970s as a junior Quantity Surveyor, I was introduced to the '*frozen feet, hot head*' experience of uninsulated site cabins, with their austere, bleak and unwelcoming dirt-grey work environment. Fast forward, and today we have insulated cabins with PIR sensors, and very occasionally you come across plants within the site cabin, windows providing decent daylight or sparks of innovation like free fresh fruit for site personnel provided daily. But generally the internal working environment on site hasn't changed much since the 1970s. Even co-location spaces on large projects are often tucked away in the bowels of a building with no daylight. We tend to think of these offices as temporary, but '*temporary*' can be anything up to a few years, and many site personnel spend whole careers in temporary accommodation.

Consider the traditional construction site manager, typical of those managing buildings up and down the country, day in, day out. Commuting to site is in heavy, stressful traffic, often in poor light, for considerable distances. The day is spent in those dirt-grey cabins, or basement areas with poor strip lighting, inadequate daylight, heating or ventilation, only to travel home once more in poor light and heavy traffic. Five or six days a week. Fifty weeks a year.

Construction project accommodation is in need of urgent review. It was encouraging to hear that the safety officer of a subcontractor working on a recent well known London landmark construction project prohibited their staff from using the allocated shared and open plan project office area. Located on the second floor of the construction project, the office had no daylight, no views, no greenery, and continuous strip lighting, and the ban was on the grounds that these were unhealthy working conditions. When allocating temporary accommodation, the main contractor should have applied the same healthy building values it was providing in the finished building.

Facilities managers are often treated similarly – housed in basements, areas shared with services, or light-locked rooms in the middle of buildings. Where, then, is the exposure to nature, the healthy environments that we promote when designing and bidding for new buildings, when it comes to the project management of sites? Surely this is a key area to improve the health, creativity and image of our industry.

The 'health' of the construction or facilities management's environment is a key area for clients to address though procurement, and for sustainability schemes such as CCS, BREEAM, LEED, JUST, Well, LBC and LPC to assess in greater detail.

It can be done, through a strategy that focuses on 'greening the site office' to create high-performance construction workspaces and boost construction staff health and wellbeing. For example, Brookfield Multiplex in partnership with '202020 Vision' at Wetherill Park in New South Wales, noted as Australia's first green construction site, is '*bringing the greening concept into the site office*'.

Lauren Haas, Brookfield's Australian sustainability manager, commented: '*We envisage seeing the same or better improvements in our own staff that is integral to delivering high performance buildings for our clients as well as being an employer of choice.*' [14]

SALUTOGENESIS

Literally meaning '*the generation of health*', salutogenesis describes an approach that focuses on factors supporting human health and wellbeing, as well as on factors that cause ill health. An understanding of salutogenesis can help us progress towards net-postive health thinking within the built environment.

PERSPECTIVE
THE CONCEPT OF SALUTOGENESIS
SOO DOWNE,
PROFESSOR IN MIDWIFERY STUDIES AT UCLAN

The concept of salutogenesis was developed by Aaron Antonovsky, a medical sociologist, while he was undertaking research with older women who were survivors of Nazi concentration camps. He expected to find high levels of psychological pathology in these survivors, and, indeed, this was the case for many of them. However, he was surprised to find that a small minority retained a positive outlook on life, despite all the traumas they had endured. He began to wonder how people could endure such extreme horrors, and still maintain a positive outlook. He also began to question the focus on pathology which permeates much of healthcare research and practice, and public health philosophy. These reflections led him to the theory of *salutogenesis*, or the '*generation of wellbeing*' (Antonovsky 1979, 1987).[15]

Salutogenesis maintains that human beings exist on a spectrum – from death at one end to full and healthy life on the other – and that we all move along this spectrum, in both directions, throughout our lives. Antonovsky was particularly interested in the potential for the promotion of wellbeing at the 'healthy' end of this spectrum, to balance the strong professional and sociopolitical emphasis on ill health at the negative end of the spectrum. He developed the concept of the sense of coherence (SOC). This includes three key parameters: manageability, comprehensibility and meaningfulness.

More broadly, salutogenesis has come to mean an orientation towards the maintenance or generation of positive attributes in general, in contrast to focusing on negative circumstances or outcomes. This has been utilised in a range of contexts, both within and beyond health. For example, emergent groups such as the Healthy Settings movement, alongside others interested in building design and urban spaces and health outcomes, have integrated Antonovsky's original observations on what maintains health into concerns about the environment and living spaces, thereby uniting concerns with space, place and wellbeing within a broadly salutogenic framework (Dooris et al 2007, Mitchell et al 2011).[16]

Rethinking Health

This turn towards the positive, healthy end of the spectrum of human life and activity has yet to be explored fully. We need a net-positive health shift in thinking in the built environment, moving the focus away from the causes of illness to the causes of health. We have to consider health issues as part of the performance gap, closing the loop between desired health improvement design considerations and those actually achieved. This applies to the design of homes and buildings, the refurbishment and facilities management of existing buildings, and occupational health and safety thinking as it relates to construction and manufacturing activities.

A recent World Green Build Council publication, *Better Places for People*, illustrated a range of innovative projects, demonstrating benefits of healthy, sustainable buildings that are making the lives of occupants and visitors better. These include the Marks & Spencer Cheshire Oaks green store and British Land's refurbishment at its London York House head office.[17]

AND SO TO BIOPHILIA

'We will have the ability in a very short time to create buildings that are literally as complex as a plant or a flower, that are biophilic in the true sense of the word.'

PAUL HAWKEN[18]

The term biophilia was coined by E. O. Wilson his book of that name.[19] Literally meaning 'love of nature', the term suggests a deep, innate affinity between humans and nature. Biophilic design is the theory, the science and the practice of bringing buildings 'alive', recognising and improving bonds with nature. It is a response to the human desire to re-establish our contact with nature within built environments.

As an example, researcher Roger Ulrich found that patients whose hospital window overlooked nature recorded shorter post-operative stays, required less pain medication and, interestingly, evaluated their nurses more positively after gall bladder surgery than patients who looked onto a brick wall (Ulrich, 1984).[20]

Stephen Kellert's seminal *Biophilic Design: The Theory, Science and Practice of Bringing Buildings to Life* defined biophilia in this context as '*building and landscape design that enhances human physical and mental wellbeing by fostering positive connections between people and nature.*'[21] Kellert recognised that the prevailing approach to building design encourages a massive transformation and degradation of natural systems along with an increased isolation from nature that results in '*unsustainable energy and resource consumption, major biodiversity loss, pollution and contamination*', and more. Yet, as Kellert commented, we have designed ourselves into this situation.

We can design ourselves out of it, but only through a *'radically different paradigm'* that seeks harmonisation with nature. Biophilic design is that missing link in prevailing approaches to sustainable building design.

Leading biophilia advocates Terrapin Bright Green, a New York-based environmental and planning consultancy engaged in conversations and innovations for sustainability opportunities, published *14 Patterns of Biophilic Design*.[22] Whilst written for use during the design of buildings, it equally applies to workspace considerations in offices and temporary construction accommodation; it is an essential guide and primer to incorporating biophilia in the built environment.

NATURE IN THE SPACE PATTERNS

1 Visual connection with nature
2 Non-visual connection with nature
3 Non-rhythmic sensory stimuli
4 Thermal and airflow variability
5 Presence of water
6 Dynamic and diffuse light
7 Connection with natural systems

NATURAL ANALOGUES PATTERNS

8 Biomorphic forms and patterns
9 Material connection with nature
10 Complexity and order

NATURE OF THE SPACE PATTERNS

11 Prospect
12 Refuge
13 Mystery
14 Risk/peril

Figure 3.1 Fourteen patterns of biophilic design

However, benefits from biophilic design are not limited to building interiors, as Joe Clancy, project landscape architect and LBC UK Collaborative member commented on the Human Spaces blog:

PERSPECTIVE
VIEWS TO NATURE
JOE CLANCY,
LANDSCAPE ARCHITECT AND BIOPHILIC DESIGNER

With restrictions on the forms of biophilic design that can be accommodated in interior settings, external views to nature become necessary to establish interior restorative environments. However, creating external views to nature is pointless if there is no nature. A designer may accommodate external views through nearby windows for occupants to create a biophilic environment, but landscape architects play a vital role in creating those same views. Occupants respond more strongly to views of nature than to the natural analogues which are used to a large degree in interior settings, as our brains can tell the difference between representational and 'actual' nature. So in practice, landscape architecture has a role to play in creating biophilic environments inside and out.

ECO-GOVERNANCE AND RESPONSIBILITY

One question has been continuously framing and re-framing itself in my mind throughout writing this book. Where is the soul of built environment sustainability? *Is* there a soul? What does the question even mean? Does it even matter?

Indeed, it is fair to say, an organisation cannot truly deliver sustainability through the commissioning, design, construction or maintenance of buildings unless sound sustainability values form its core governance and culture.

Eco-Governance Driving the Triple Bottom Line

We have become very familiar with the triple bottom line approach to sustainability and corporate social responsibility, i.e. environment, society and economic. It forms the basis of many environmental and sustainability visions, policy statements and development initiatives. In the business arena, this is the acknowledged responsible '*bottom line*' of meeting economic goals (usually growth and profit) while also meeting environmental goals (reducing impact) and social goals (addressing community issues) in carrying out business activities.

Triple bottom line thinking can be traced back to Patrick Geddes.[23] Now recognised as the grandfather of town and country planning, Geddes coined the triptych '*Place, folk and work*'. In its current form, however, it is credited to John Elkington and his 1998 book *Cannibals with Forks: The Triple Bottom Line of 21st Century Business.*[24]

While we can easily identify Geddes' '*Place*' as being the '*Environment*' circle in a Venn diagram (interestingly, the Living Building Challenge renamed its '*Site*' petal as '*Place*' for version 3) and the '*Work*' aspect is readily identified as the '*Economy*' circle, there is an uneasy fit with people or '*Folk*' in the '*Society*' circle. Are staff part of society, and where do the governance arrangements of a business (including the ISO 9001-related quality and organisational arrangements/controls vital for sustainability) fit into the three circles of sustainability?

Is There a Quad Bottom Line?

The quadruple bottom line introduces governance as a fourth bottom line. Governance, or culture, is defined here as including the formal business, administrative and 'control' processes of an organisation, as well as the informal networks, traditions and cultural and behavioural norms which act as enablers or disablers of sustainable development.

Figure 3.2 **The quadruple bottom line**

Sustainability governance includes those organisational items that are vital enablers for sustainable development. Many are embedded within the modern sustainability building programmes such as the Living Building Challenge, JUST and the WELL Building Standard.

The governance leaf on the sustainability Venn diagram raises both important questions and huge opportunities for advancing sustainability development, as well as providing structure for a new generation of more ecologically holistic sustainability thinking.

Figure 3.3 Governance: Enablers for sustainability

SUSTAINABLE DEVELOPMENT GOALS

The UN Sustainable Development Goals,[25] signed off in 2015, are not just for adoption by individual countries, but can and will form eco-governance drivers for organisations, who, if serious, will adopt natural and social capital reporting alongside financial reporting, thereby strengthening the triple bottom line approach.

We will see many organisations embrace the goals as a foundation and vision for sustainability and corporate social responsibility strategies, replacing the Brundtland

definition of 'doing nothing today to compromise future generations'.

Figure 3.4 The UN sustainable development goals[26]

ECO-GOVERNANCE AND CSR
Tools available to us for shaping, guiding and monitoring our eco-governance.

EFQM (sustainability)	In 2004 the European Foundation for Quality Management (EFQM) published a CSR version, addressing the three dimensions of CSR (social, environment and economic), aligning the nine criteria of the Excellence Framework with those of the Global Compact. This has now been updated to the *EFQM Framework for Sustainability*.[27]
Global Reporting Initiative	Global Reporting Initiative[28] is an independent organisation that '*helps businesses, governments and other organisations understand and communicate the impact of business on critical sustainability issues such as climate change, human rights, corruption and many others*'.
JUST	The ILFI's JUST Programme,[29] aligned to the Living Building Challenge (where it is a requirement for at least one member of a project team to be JUST-registered), is a '*call to social justice action*'. It is a CSR programme, described as a transparency programme to reveal social, financial and environmental approaches and performance.
Living Product Challenge	The Living Product Challenge,[30] based on Living Building Challenge philosophy, '*re-imagines the design and construction of products to function as elegantly and efficiently as anything found in the natural world*'. The LPC standard supports the construction manufacturers' journey towards regenerative sustainability in both their products and organisation.
BCorp	BCorp's[31] B-Lab certification is a third party standard requiring companies to meet social sustainability, environmental performance and accountability standards, and to be transparent to the public.
Business in the Community	Business in the Community[32] is the Prince's Responsible Business Network. Members work together to tackle a wide range of issues that are essential to creating a fairer society and a more sustainable future.

ISO 26001	ISO 26001,[33] the International Standard for Corporate Responsibility, provides guidance on how businesses and organisations can operate in a socially responsible way, acting in an ethical and transparent way that contributes to the health and welfare of society.
ISO 14001:2015	The ISO 14001:2015[34] edition of the environmental management standard raises the corporate environment governance issue, for example requiring that 'top management' and organisational 'risks and opportunities' become part of everyday environmental management.

RESPONSIBLE CONTRACTING

What if assessment schemes such as the UK Considerate Construction Scheme could make the flip, rewarding contractors doing more good, not just less bad, at project level? The scheme considers environmental issues as part of its remit to improve the image of construction, and quite rightly so. However, having got the full attention of the UK construction sector, it has become a key influencer and motivator, and consequently must embrace that responsibility, recognising a great opportunity to replace 'business as usual' sustainability with a greener, deeper restorative sustainability – one that is ecologically and socially just.

With most reasonable construction projects now scoring 7 or 8 out of 10 for environmental performance, and receiving certifications of achievement for being just 'less bad', many projects and contractors now seeing themselves as somehow 'beyond compliant' and ask why do more?

Many organisations are looking for a wider recognition of environmental and social responsibility governance and deployment, often through industry, and cross sector environmental and social awards. In addition, programmes such as JUST, the international BCorp and the GRI (Global Reporting Initiative) bring a fresh approach to responsible business that looks attractive to industry leaders.

PERSPECTIVE
RESPONSIBLE CONSTRUCTION STRATEGY
GUY PARKER,
MANAGING DIRECTOR, CONLON CONSTRUCTION

Conlon Construction's Responsible Construction Strategy has been inspired and shaped around the philosophy and advocacy of the Living Building Challenge. Coupled with our pursuit of JUST label acknowledgement and ISO 26001, we believe this provides a powerful framework representing a cutting edge in construction – one that firmly embraces the more traditional corporate social responsibility approaches of donations, volunteering and school visits, but also moves beyond that.

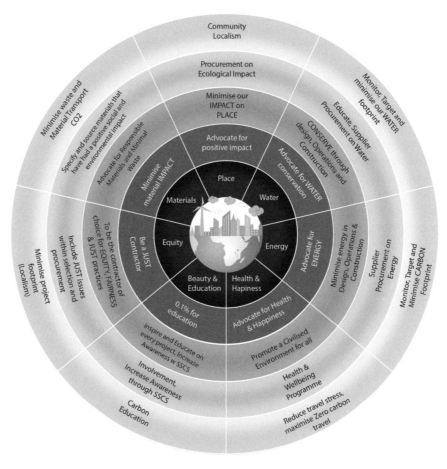

Figure 3.5 Conlon Construction's Responsible Construction Strategy [35]
SSCS is Supply Chain Sustainability School

RESTORATIVE EDUCATION

Part of our responsibility must be to inspire the next generation to become better than us and to reach higher than we have. Every project has a responsibility to educate and inspire the next generation, the next project, the next innovation.

It is perhaps beyond the scope of this book[36] to explore in detail how sustainability is taught in construction courses and degrees, but my experience of working with a number of academic institutions tells me it is by no means embedded deep enough within the curricula. Those in industry also have a huge influencing role to play. Education and eco-literacy is one of the more powerful tools in our restorative sustainability toolbox, yet it is often overlooked.

As Christine Mondor of EvolveEA, a Living Building Challenge advocate herself, noted in a recent conversation for this book, *'Training is shaped as a technical offering, and considered by many (in the built environment) as all we are licensed to do. We therefore feel uncomfortable with the inclusion of social and equity issues within building certification schemes, and uncomfortable in promoting to clients, designing and constructing from social perspectives.'*[37]

Mondor is an architect very much at the forefront of restorative sustainability, seeing the Living Building Challenge as a philosophy far greater than its parts. She is an advocate for inclusivity and social responsibility; her architectural practice is a registered BCorp and Women Owned organisation. Reflecting on the social influence of the built environment, Christine commented, *'Equity is cast from the power structures of the built environment.'*

There is a real need for people with vision, Christine told me – not for quick wins that we can get with the traditional green standards like LEED and BREEAM which offer a snapshot at design and at end of construction. Instead, she favours philosophies that are *through time*, that foster long-term thinking and relationships, and that recognise the need to collaboratively grow into that philosophy.

And those long-term mutual relationships go way beyond the project team, to include the community and to understand relationships with nature and the environment.

Understanding health within the built environment needs to be firmly established as part of sustainability education and as a common health issue. It should teach us how to operate and live in homes, but also the provision of healthy buildings, free of toxic material. As Fionn Stevenson commented at a recent RIBA event on healthy buildings, *'Health practitioners can be "agents of change" for sustainability within Architecture curriculums.'*[38]

Homebase, the UK DIY chain, has worked with biophilia advocate and consultant Oliver Heath to develop its Life Improvement educational material.[39] Its aim is to 'recategorise' DIY from home improvement to life improvement, in recognition of the need to improve health and wellbeing in the home. It's hugely commendable – but this is the awareness and knowledge that should be within education curriculums, and included, for example, within the 'operation and maintenance' manuals handed over to new building owners and occupants following construction works.

Many projects and project teams have engaged with education organisations in the name of considerate construction or social, responsible construction, establishing and improving relationships between schools and the project. While this is beneficial to schools, we can and should give more meaning and structure to these initiatives. Many school outreach relationships are driven by client or project requirements, and many projects and organisations who would be identified as part of the 'accommodationist culture' would not engage with schools if not required to do so.

Where these engagements take place they are most likely to be managed by the main contractor, with very little project team or supply chain engagement. When was the last time a mechanical or electrical contractor participated?

Restorative Education – at Secondary, University and Postgraduate levels

'Hands on engagement in sustainable design, at a youthful age, can produce a generation of leaders with the necessary vision and skills to build a new, hopeful world.'

DENIS HAYES [40]

Structure and meaning for introducing sustainability thinking into secondary schools can be achieved through schemes such as the inspiring Design... Engineer... Construct! (DEC) programme delivered by Class Of Your Own.

PERSPECTIVE
DESIGN... ENGINEER... CONSTRUCT!
ALISON WATSON,
MANAGING DIRECTOR OF CLASS OF YOUR OWN

Young people are always asking why we learn. Encouraging their curiosity, creativity and innovation, and giving them the medium to apply their knowledge of STEM subjects (science, technology, engineering and maths), is paramount. The vast, exciting industry that is the built environment offers young people opportunities, to be creative and innovative.

Design... Engineer... Construct! (DEC) is an accredited learning programme for secondary-school students, developed to create the next generation of built environment professionals. Through a project-based approach, DEC applies pure academic subjects to the latest construction industry practices. The result: young people with practical experience and employability skills.

There is little understanding of built environment professions at school level, and few young people aspire to a career in this important sector of the British and global economy. By getting involved with DEC, schools and industry can shape the future of construction and change the lives of young people.

With the support of industry leaders, professional bodies and progressive universities, DEC delivers an inspiring programme that is up to date and in demand by the very people who will employ our children.

PERSPECTIVE
UNIVERSITY DESIGN COMPETITIONS
JENNI BARRETT,
SENIOR LECTURER, SCHOOL OF ARCHITECTURE, UCLAN

The UCLAN Midge Hole Living Building Design Competition involved working for a client and on complex and isolated terrain, Masters in Architecture students at UCLan (the University of Central Lancashire) pioneered the values of the Living Building Challenge within the UK. Facilitated by Martin Brown with support and guidance from Living Future ambassadors globally, via social media and web feeds, students explored the future of domestic living in an architecture that seeks to go far beyond current sustainable thinking, creating an innovative design solution for the competition client, while embracing the rigorous LBC standards.[41]

PERSPECTIVE
REGENERATION
CARLO BATTISTI,
LIVING BUILDING CHALLENGE AMBASSADOR

REGENERATION was the first design competition in Europe entirely based on the Living Building Challenge protocol. The 64-hour non-stop European contest launched in 2015 by MDS was to develop a project of sustainable requalification, 'regenerating' a public building in Dro (Trentino, Italy). Fifteen professionals under the age of 35 from all over Europe participated; divided into three multidisciplinary teams, their task was to regenerate the Municipality of Dro's building, meeting the need for new spaces for associations and young people, reorganisation of the library, connection to the river Sarca and transforming the building for the benefit of future generations. The result would be a kind of living organism (a 'Living Building'), completely autonomous in its use of resources, and harmoniously integrated into the natural environment and the village. The purpose of the competition was to show the best sustainable regeneration project in terms of architecture, energy efficiency, livability and relationship with social, urban and natural context.

The title REGENERATION is a tribute to the first 'generation' of young professionals (architects, engineers) whose ideas can start to 'regenerate' the built environment, achieving the best possible performances for the single building. The second REGENERATION competition took place in April 2016.

The winning project showed not only that the time is ripe to consolidate in a very efficient way our built environment – without settling for 'a bit less consuming' solutions – but also that a generation of young professionals is ready to meet this challenge in a radically innovative and effective way.

More than 80 people from all over Italy attended the competition's public conference, showing that many designers, public administrators and companies are ready to follow these 'pioneers'. LBC expert speakers from the US and Europe opened our eyes to a future of 'regenerated' cities. These communities won't be satisfied with merely 'doing less harm to the environment', but will actually combine respect for nature, social equity and a sustainable economy.

COLLABORATION
– SUSTAINABILITY WITHOUT BARRIERS

We now have nearly 100 years of collaborative efforts in the built environment sector, from Alfred Bossom and skyscrapers (*Building for the Skies*, published in 1934) to today's Construction 2025 strategy. Throughout this period the focus for collaboration has been on 'delivering superior value' – to the client, end users and on the supply side. And although we have had moderate success in this, the trends are not good. Projects finish farther behind schedule in 2015 than they did in 2000, and there is little movement in customer satisfaction.

Today's projects have new stakeholders, requiring new relationships with the community and with the environment. We need new collaborative thinking, for what Hannah Jones of Nike called new, unconventional collaborations. As the old African proverb goes: '*If you want to go fast, go alone; if you want to go far, go together.*'

Collaboration 2025

FUTURE COLLABORATIONS FOR A RESTORATIVE FUTURE WILL BE …	
Holistic	Not only seen as project-focused, but as part of the community and connected to 'place' and the environment.
Net positive	Moving from a managing compliance and risk culture to one that seeks net-positive solutions.
Sharing	'Sharership' collaboration in the age of social media: informing, inspiring the project and advocating far beyond.
Digital	Collaboration as an enabler in the age of BIM.
Lean	Collaboration with the last planner, throughout the supply chain, removing Muda (wastefulness).
Unconventional	Collaboration that adds value through unconventional supply chains. Communities of Practice that collaborate for built environment innovation across organisations.

To achieve collaboration for sustainability we have to remove the barriers and baggage that the built environment has built, hoarded and been restricted by over the last few decades. Undoubtedly BIM will help in this – but without collaboration, BIM, while an important tool in our toolbox, will be misused or remain, partially used.

Building Down Barriers, a 1990's built environment collaborative action research programme, provided us with a set of principles for adding value through collaboration and supply chain integration.[42]

These principles strongly correlate with how we should collaborate through BIM to work together in a digital age. They also provide us with a set of guidelines for providing 'superior sustainability value' through collaboration and integration.

SUSTAINABLE BUILDING WITHOUT BARRIERS

Deliver superior value	Establish a net-positive vision for ecologically and socially just sustainability.
Establish long-term relationships	Establish through-time relationships with stakeholders, innovators and communities who can deliver restorative sustainability.
Integrate services	Collaborative sharing and circular economy thinking.
Collaboratively manage costs	Collaboratively manage the triple bottom line costs of restorative sustainability.
Continuous improvement	Facilitate improvement, going beyond zero targets for ever increasing net-positive benefits.
People and leadership	Be role models, advocating and providing awareness and resources for regenerative sustainability.

RESTORATIVE VALUE

> Imagine if every value-engineering exercise made the world a better place.

The concept of value within the built environment has always been a thorny issue, in understanding the questions of what constitutes value, to whom it is valuable, and what exactly is 'added value'. *Be Valuable* by Richard Saxon provided a sound treaty on the topic and has remained a good reference, or at least a starting reference, as the world has changed.[43] The mix or blend of value today is far different from that in 2000, but it is rarely expressed in an ecological or social language of love, nature or compassion.

Value management and engineering exercises – the manner in which value and function is brought into project decision-making – were initially founded on traditional project stakeholders, and focused on value in terms of financial returns, programmes and quality. The VM and VE exercises I led in the late 1990s blended the different wants and the wide spectrum of values from the different groups of stakeholders. But with 'value' today having new dimensions – including social and ecological ones – the understanding of how to optimise a new mix of value within any decision-making process will emerge as a key skill. This will and must change the way we approach value management and value engineering exercises.

Value engineering exercises take place day in, day out across the industry, more often than not to reduce cost (and, by doing so, increasing environmental and societal impact). But imagine if the purpose of VE was to reduce *impact* rather than cost. Arguably, through reducing impact we are reducing costs at some point in the project life cycle and enabling wider triple bottom line thinking.

A new style of value management approach based on restorative working does succeed. It brings the stakeholders together, along with the voice of the community and the environment, as has been demonstrated in design charrettes for possible Living Building Challenge Projects in the UK.

	RESTORATIVE VALUE
Value management	The *strategic*-level exercise of maximising the project's net-positive sustainability capability. Defining and establishing the sustainability philosophy and vision for the project
Value engineering	The *operational*-level exercise of maximising the project's net-positive sustainability function of a building, component or process. Ensuring design and operational decisions remain focused on the projects restorative sustainability philosophy and vision.

MIND-FULL OR MINDFUL?

Running throughout this chapter's thread of rethinking, of changing mindsets, is the importance of approaching sustainability in the built environment with a different perspective, and a different language. Key to this rethinking is the concept of mindfulness. Once the domain of transcendental meditation and Buddhism, mindfulness is now increasingly considered key in business rethinking.

Mindfulness is fast gathering pace as a set of practices to manage stress or to enhance daily living 'in the present moment'. Organisations large and small, including those in the construction sector, are starting to explore how mindfulness can aid wellbeing, sustainability and improved organisational success. Zen masters such as Thich Nhat Hanh have become highly sought mindfulness gurus for global technology organisations such as Google.

At present we have minds full of stress and worry, of technical perspectives. In business, we use a language of competition and war, of technology, that leaves little room for the language of love, passion and caring. And this is reflected in our approach to sustainable design, construction and operation.

PERSPECTIVE
THE HUMAN INNER ENVIRONMENT IMPACT ON THE BUILT ENVIRONMENT
ANNE PARKER,
COACH, PROJECT MANAGER, MINDFULNESS PRACTITIONER

OK, I see your amazing new project. Your eco-sustainable, living-materials, planet-friendly building. It beams out at me from the journals – your PR people have done a great job. It shines, it beams, it blows my socks off. Now I'm looking at one of your project managers. And I look again, a little more closely. Now the light is not so bright, now the beam is not so strong. I am looking at fractured thoughts, disturbed sleep, skipped meals. I'm looking at ever-present simmering levels of irritability, of intolerance, of impatience, of short attention spans, of reduced focus, a shadow of pessimism, ongoing anxiety and a mind that never stops.

Is this the best human intelligence? Is this sustainable? Is the building or the project really worth this?

Are we so disingenuous that we can't build amazing projects that are also affirming to the human spirit, and to the finest energies of human functioning? To the energies of joy and inspiration?

More and more people in the construction industry are turning to mindfulness as a way of grounding themselves in the face of increasing pressures that fire on them from every direction. The jargon about 'the bottom line', meaning project profit, is millions of miles from the real bottom line, which is human death from the inside. No one has a problem understanding construction death from trips, slips and falls or coffins being delivered to football stadia projects – but who is noting the number of individuals dying from the inside out from the lives of their jobs?

You may want to call it 'stress'. I don't – because an absence of stress still does not capture the most exquisite properties of human creativity and enthusiasm, the joy of an individual who has some inner 'space' from which they can draw every day and put new depth and quality into what they do.

Early work is being done on the energy within spaces, built or otherwise. There will be a tumultuous day of awakening when the realisation is made that the quality of all human life involved in any built environment project is absolutely endemic to its success as a space, and I work for this day. It has started and it is thrilling and exciting. Thank you to all who are working on themselves inside in order to improve and strengthen what they do on the outside.

As Jo Confino, former *Guardian* Sustainable Business director and now with the *Huffington Post*, has stated often – most recently in connection with the Volkswagen carbon dioxide fiasco[44] – business needs to learn, or re-learn, the language of love. It must move away from a language of war ('*fighting for market share*'), of competition and fear (of '*losing out*' to others). With perhaps one of the most profound observations on mindfulness in relation to business and sustainability, he comments that we judge love as having no place in business. Love is seen as a weakness. '*But love is the strongest power we can muster,*' Confino counters, arguing that love can enable us to '*produce goods and services that make the world a better place*', enable businesses to better manage responsibility, treat people and the planet with respect, and be answerable to our children without guilt.

Perhaps, this significantly adds to the understanding of where or what is the soul of built environment sustainability.

1   Executive Secretary of the UN Framework Convention on Climate Change (UNFCCC): see TEDTalk http://blog.ted.com/impossible-isnt-a-fact-its-an-attitude-christiana-figueres-at-ted2016
2   Pope Francis's encyclical *Laudato Si*' (2015), subtitled 'On Care For Our Common Home', http://w2.vatican.va/content/francesco/en/encyclicals/documents/papa-francesco_20150524_enciclica-laudato-si.html
3   http://www.theguardian.com/books/2015/feb/27/robert-macfarlane-word-hoard-rewilding-landscape
4   Zelenski, J.M. et al., Journal of Environmental Psychology, Carleton University, Ottawa, Canada.
5   Zelenski, J.M., Dopko, R.L, and C.A. Capaldi, *Cooperation is in our nature: Nature exposure may promote cooperative and environmentally sustainable behavior:* http://colincapaldi.weebly.com/uploads/3/8/9/5/38959019/cooperation_is_in_our_nature.pdf
6   Video link: https://vimeo.com/152803075
7   http://www.bbc.co.uk/news/science-environment-33959562
8   Dyson Centre for Neonatal Care: http://www.dezeen.com/2011/08/08/the-dyson-centre-for-neonatal-care-by-feilden-clegg-bradley-studios/
9   Childbirth Overtreatment Projects: https://www.ariadnelabs.org/childbirth-projects
10 'Asthma could be worsened by energy-efficient homes, warns study': http://www.theguardian.com/society/2015/sep/20/energy-efficient-homes-could-worsen-asthma
11 http://www.dailymail.co.uk/sciencetech/article-2358191/OAPs-die-Green-Deal-homes-Energy-saving-scheme-leave-homes-dangerously-overheated.html (Accessed 2015)
12 'NHS to help create "healthy new towns"': http://www.bbc.co.uk/news/health-35687296?utm_content=buffer90055&utm_medium=social&utm_source=twitter.com&utm_campaign=buffer
13 https://www.academia.edu/2456916/Salutogenic_design_The_neural_basis_for_health_promoting_environments
14 http://www.architectureanddesign.com.au/news/australia-s-first-green-construction-site
15 Antonovsky, A., *Health, Stress and Coping*, San Francisco, Jossey-Bass Publishers, 1979. Antonovsky, A., *Unraveling The Mystery of Health – How People Manage Stress and Stay Well*, San Francisco, Jossey-Bass Publishers, 1987.
16 Dooris, M.T. et al., 'Healthy Settings: Building evidence for the effectiveness of whole system health promotion – challenges and future directions', in *Global Perspectives on Health Promotion Effectiveness*, Springer Verlag, 2007, pp.327–52. Mitchell, R., Astell-Burt, T. and E.A. Richardson, A comparison of green space indicators for epidemiological research. *Journal of Epidemiology and Community Health*, 65 (10). 853-858, 2011.
17 Better Places for People, World Green Building Council: www.worldgbc.org
18 *Trim Tab – International Living Future Institute Journal*, vol.18, Summer 2013: http://living-future.org/news/trim-tab-v18-out

19   Wilson, E.O., *Biophilia*, Cambridge MA, Harvard University Press, 1984.

20   Ulrich, R., 'View through a window may influence recovery from surgery', 1984: https://mdc.mo.gov/sites/default/files/resources/2012/10/ulrich.pdf

21   Kellert, S.R., Heerwagen, J. and M. Mador, *Biophilic Design: The Theory, Science and Practice of Bringing Buildings to Life*, John Wiley & Sons, ISBN 0470163348, 2008.

22   *14 Patterns of Biophilic Design Terrapin Bright Green:* http://www.terrapinbrightgreen.com/wp-content/uploads/2014/09/14-Patterns-of-Biophilic-Design-Terrapin-2014p.pdf

23   Patrick Geddes: http://www.nls.uk/learning-zone/politics-and-society/patrick-geddes

24   Elkington, J., *Cannibals with Forks: The Triple Bottom Line of 21st Century Business,* New Society Publishers, ISBN 0865713928, 1998.

25   https://sustainabledevelopment.un.org/post2015/transformingourworld

26   Credit: http://www.unmultimedia.org/radio/english/wp-content/uploads/2016/01/sdg-poster.jpg

27   EFQM Framework for Sustainability: http://www.efqm.org/efqm-framework-for-sustainability

28   Global Reporting Index: https://www.globalreporting.org

29   JUST Programme: http://justorganizations.com

30   http://living-future.org/lpc

31   https://www.bcorporation.net/ and UK bcorporation.uk

32   Business in the Community: http://www.bitc.org.uk

33   ISO 26001: http://www.iso.org/iso/home/standards/iso26000.htm

34   ISO 14001:2015: http://www.iso.org/iso/catalogue_detail?csnumber=60857

35   Source: Conlon Construction

36   A Recommended bibliography and study module is provided in Chapter Eight

37   Christine Mondor, EvolveEA, Pittsburgh, PA, http://www.evolveea.com/work/christine-mondor

38   Prof Fionn Stevenson, Head of School of Architecture, The University of Sheffield. Tweeted by Hattie Hartman (AJ)

39   http://www.homebase.co.uk/en/static/life-improvement/the-theory

40   Denis Hayes, President of the Bullitt Foundation, message of support for a launch at an ambitious Class Of Your Own programme (the Institute of Design, Space and Place) in Manchester to drive sustainability thinking into the school programme by rethinking education for an ecological age, 2015

41   https://jennibarrett.wordpress.com/2014/05/12/welcome-to-midge-hole-mill

42   Building Down Barriers: http://www.ribabookshops.com/item/building-down-barriers-a-guide-to-construction-best-practice/31687

43   *Be Valuable* by Richard Saxon: http://www.saxoncbe.com/be-valuable.pdf

44   Jo Confino: 'Why Business Needs To Learn The Language Of Love': http://www.huffingtonpost.com/entry/why-does-business-find-it-so-hard-to-speak-the-language-of-love_us_560166a2e4b08820d91a1eab

CHAPTER FOUR
RESTORATIVE APPROACHES 1
NATURE, EARTH, LIGHT AND AIR

INTRODUCTION

This, and the following chapter explore innovations, inspirations and challenges for rethinking construction in the ecological age that will enable restorative and net positive futures.

Globally, we have no sustainable or resilient cities and only a small handful of truly sustainable buildings. And, despite a focus on resiliency, of those that are recognised today as sustainable buildings, very few – if any – will make sustainable sense 30 years from now, as we approach the 2050 carbon reduction milestone.

With few notable exceptions, we as a sector have had our eyes wide shut in really getting to grips with climate change and the sustainability agenda. There has been a couple of decades of building sustainability that has blindly focused on energy reduction and building efficiency, yet there are serious performance gaps that the sector has made little progress in addressing. The sustainability agenda will become more stringent, and more costly to address, if we don't act now.

If the built environment is to take responsibility for its 40% impact and play its full role in progressing towards the 1.5°C climate change future targeted in the 2015 Paris Agreement,[1] then indeed we have much to do. Not only do we have to stop being less bad, or being content with being net-positive, but we have to be very positive.

Very Positive is used here as an expression of being visibly and demonstrably positive on approaches undertaken and results attained.

This and the following chapter cover the more physical aspects and attributes for restorative future buildings, from the earth, to lighting, energy, materials and waste. It is these attributes that will be visible to building users, to funders and to the public, and will inspire other clients, designers, constructors and operations. Equally importantly, they will be a visible demonstration that we as a built environment sector can and will play our part in the climate change challenge, not continuing to contribute to the problem, or simply reducing our impact when it suits us to do so.

NATURE

> 'I'm not trying to imitate nature, I am trying to find the principles she's using.'

RICHARD BUCKMINSTER FULLER, 1972

The degree to which we recognise our interdependent relationship with nature is reflected in our approach to sustainability, and the ways in which we design, build, maintain and use buildings. As the understanding of this relationship weakens, so does our respect for nature and consequently our tolerance for doing harm increases.

With insensitive planning over the decades, as well as a focus on building isolation and insulation, a blinkered sustainability push on energy performance and increased use of smart technologies, our buildings have lost any real connection with nature.

Biomimicry

Biomimicry is based on the principle that if we really got to understand nature, then we could mimic the way nature solves problems and apply these solutions to our everyday problems, and to the built environment. Biomimicry, once seen as a revolutionary idea, has recently gained much traction and is now transforming many building designs, building components and materials. We should note that biomimicry thinking is not just confined to material innovation, but applies equally to how we project manage – learning from and mimicking how nature approaches and enables solutions.

Janice Benyus's 1998 book *Biomimicry, Innovation Inspired by Nature*[2] introduced nine principles that would go on to raise biomimicry's popularity through TED talks and social media presence and sharing. These nine principles (outlined below) describe how nature works, and how nature can contribute to our sustainability efforts. Perhaps unsurprisingly there is great resonance between these principles and the imperatives of restorative sustainability approaches and standards such as the Living Building Challenge, the WELL Building Standard and thinking emerging within BREEAM and LEED.

Michael Palwyn in his 2016 reissued *Biomimicry in Architecture*,[3] a book rich with biomimicry applications across the built environment, describes biomimicry as developing sustainable solutions that mimic the *functional basis* of nature.

Biomimicry Principles (J. Benyus)
Nature runs on sunlight: The energy of the sun powers all in nature. Relying solely on renewable energy within the built environment is now within our capabilities.

Nature uses only the energy it needs: To achieve this we need significant improvements in understanding and applying strict management for building energy use.

Nature fits form to function: Nature is appropriate to its location, as should be a building, with its function, form and scope being sensitive to the limits of its place.

Nature recycles everything: Everything in nature is biodegradable. A core cradle to cradle and circular economy principle.

Nature rewards cooperation: Nature thrives on cooperation and collaboration. We need to see buildings as clusters, communities and districts that can support, feed and share services and information.

Nature banks on diversity: Ecosystems that are rich in diversity thrive. Similarly, our buildings and green spaces need to be bioclimatically flexible and diverse in design, allowing for adaption to changes in climate.

Nature demands local expertise: Generally species in nature are limited to their specific local conditions. Buildings need to be designed for local bioclimatic conditions, using local materials, resources and skills.

Nature curbs excesses from within: Nature is self regulating appropriate to location. Buildings and the built environment can also self regulate, in terms of growth and development, through an understanding of the interrelationship with and impact on nature.

Nature taps the power of limits: Nature understands the limitations of place and resources. Through adopting circular economy, cradle to cradle and design for deconstruction approaches, the built environment can also understand and work within the power of limits.

Rewilding Buildings

Environmentalists recognised the 2015/16 floods in the north of England as a consequence, in part, of 'de-wilding' fells and rivers, in conjunction with river and city infrastructure that is not responsive but seeks to contain rivers on a defensive, cause and effect basis – essentially, fighting nature.

As described by advocate George Monbiot in his book *Feral*[4], rewilding is not just about reintroducing big predators such as the wolf or lynx, or reintroducing missing parts of any natural food chain, but about *'creating conditions that allow the emergence of natural responsiveness and development'*. This is restorative or regenerative environmentalism, not restricting what we allow nature to do. Consider for example the rewilded River Liza in the Ennerdale Valley in the Lake District. In the 1970s a commercial non-native cash crop plantation, planted on unnatural geometric shapes, today it is a natural wild valley that allows nature to flourish and copes naturally with flooding that has brought destruction to other nearby but strictly managed valleys.

We should learn from and apply rewilding thinking to our built environment, *creating the conditions* through – for example – biomimicry applications that allow (new and existing) buildings to breathe and to respond to natural and bioclimatic cycles.

We are losing or removing our natural barometers from buildings, increasingly replacing them with SMART technologies, to satisfy our blinkered focus on energy performance. In turn, this has weakened our intrinsic relationship with nature.

Net-Positive Construction

Living Building programmes challenge us to imagine every building and act of construction making the world a better place. But what if every construction site also made the world a better place? This is what is meant by *net-positive construction*: a construction sector that generates more energy, more water and more reusable resources than it consumes, returning greater benefits than the negative impacts it has traditionally had.

WHAT IF EVERY CONSTRUCTION SITE MADE THE WORLD A BETTER PLACE BY CONNECTING WITH NATURE?

1 Construction projects are net-positive

The construction project would have a net-positive impact on place, giving more back to the environment, nature, community and the neighbourhood than it takes, providing more benefit than disruption. It would use only locally sourced materials and services.

2 Construction projects are net-water-positive: sites are water cleansers

Harnessing water that falls on the building site for construction process and facilities, cleaning the remainder before discharging into drainage or natural watercourse systems, just as a tree would.

3 Construction projects are net-energy-positive: sites are energy generators

Harnessing sun and wind in conjunction with rapidly developing energy storage battery technology – not burning fuels and contributing to the problem. Every project must have an energy hierarchy that moves it from fossil fuels to renewables as primary construction energy source.

4 Construction projects are net-waste-positive

Sites use more waste and recycled material than new. Sites are zero waste.

5 Construction projects are net-carbon-positive

Sites are carbon net-positive. Strict carbon planning and management is key, with approaches such as living walls for site hoardings. Remaining carbon emissions after all carbon management improvements have been made are addressed with restorative offset programmes.

6 Construction projects are net-health-positive

Sites are a delight to work on, improving the health and creativity of those that work or visit. If we are really serious about *doing no harm* then we should be advocating, specifying and procuring only materials and equipment that are bio-inspired, natural, chemical-free and healthy – net-positive. The concept of COSHH (Control of Substances Hazardous to Health) needs to become seen as as dated as the use of asbestos.

7 Construction projects are lean-net-efficient-positive: everything we do goes into everything we do and more

Bio-inspired efficient construction through collaboration and knowledge sharing are key to may species. Quality is instinctive, failure and reworking rare. We learn from and adapt to complexity theory-based adaptive systems, by, for example, establishing simple rules for construction behaviour on site: *'Be Net-Positive'*, *'Do No Harm'*, *'Collaborate'*.

8 Construction projects are net-knowledge-positive

Projects share more than they learn. It is encouraging to see blogs, project Twitter accounts, videos, tours and demonstrations becoming more common. However, just as we know now that forests are linked by an underground system, a wood-wide web of mycelium that communicates information about disease, weather, water, drought and nutrient availability, so construction projects should be linked with a *well*-wide web that communicates good news, best practice and lessons learnt, using smart IoT-automated, BIM-related knowledge transfer. It should be the way we do construction.

Habitat Exchange

The Living Building Challenge includes an imperative for a habitat exchange, based on the need to restoratively address the impact that a building, in construction and through its life, will have. Discussions with potential Living Building Challenge project teams in the UK on this imperative raise the usual concerns of where, how and who (and *'what are the legal issues?'*), but chiefly centre on the additional cost of offsetting a parcel of land in perpetuity away from the project.

We could see protecting areas of wilderness and habitat exchange thinking become part of the overall restorative sustainable development package, and a key element in our corporate social responsibilities. We now recognise and accept the significant and negative impact the built environment has placed on the natural environment over many decades; not only should we be addressing immediate impacts on a project by project basis, but we should also take positive action to protect other habitats in recognition of past damage and helping to heal the future.

As a recent Cambridge University study[5] shows, rewilding and restoration of land would create carbon sinks to sequester carbon – through, for example, an increase in forestry to 30% (closer to that of France and Germany) and restoration of 700,000 hectares of peatland – and in doing so make a significant contribution to the UK's target of an 80% reduction in CO_2 emissions by 2050.

If we are serious about restorative sustainability, then habitat exchange – either physically, or through effective advocacy and/or offset programmes – should be seen as part of the cost of construction. In the context of project costs, this is likely to be less than the cost of waste (the Muda we saw in Chapter 1) on any given project.

Restorative Demonstrations

Designed by Adam Khan as part of a RIBA design competition, the visitor centre at **Brockholes Wetland and Woodland Nature Reserve, near Preston in Lancashire** is a BREEAM Outstanding cluster of floating buildings. Completed in 2011, it has established a close relationship with nature, in materials and siting. The floating buildings respond to up to 400mm fluctuations in water levels, and the roof and cladding materials (oak shakes rough-formed from tree stumps which would otherwise have been treated as waste) change colour with the changing daylight throughout the day and across the seasons.

Designed to inspire and encourage people to visit the site and engage with nature, and situated close to M6 junction 32, it provides perhaps the world's best motorway break.

'The experience is not one of the building or of nature alone, but of the two together, and comes from a certain openness: to what was already on the site, to its possibilities, to ancient and modern materials, to high and low technology.'[6]

Figure 4.1 Brockholes Visitor Centre, Lancashire

THE EARTH

'A nation that destroys its soils destroys itself.'

FRANKLIN D. ROOSEVELT

In his *Sand County Almanac*[7], Aldo Leopold, probably one of the most influential ecology authors, commented that we feel OK in abusing the land because we regard it as a *commodity* that belongs to us. He proposed '*that land as a community is the basic concept of ecology.*' Leopold's now famous '*land ethic*' philosophy valued balancing human activity on the land with natural processes.

Recently, however, in the built environment soil has become a cost inconvenience and a problem. We have downgraded the significance of soil, renaming it as mud, muck and dirt to be removed, transported and dumped, at the lowest cost and the nearest location, even if ecologically unsuitable. We then replace that soil with a different soil, imported at the end of the works, again at the lowest cost, irrespective and ignorant of the ecological or biological significance of the soil itself.

Restorative Potentials

If managed ecologically, the amount of earth works undertaken in relation to construction, through landscaping and infrastructure projects, could provide us with an easy win, offsetting many carbon emissions from the construction phase and building in use period. Rather than reliance on costly, high-tech solutions to address climate change, perhaps a key solution is right under our feet, under and around our buildings: working with the soil, not against it.

Denis Hayes, president of the Bullitt Foundation, has a lovely passage in his book *Cowed* that illustrates the importance and function of soils in reducing global warming. It illustrates why we need to pay it far more respect as an extension to our sustainability and responsible construction approaches. '*Plants and earthworms are key players in building soil. Plants draw energy from the sun through photosynthesis. They pull carbon dioxide from the air and tuck it into carbon containing packets of carbohydrates. Some of the carbon goes into plants, roots where friendly fungi and soil microbes latch onto it and store it in the form of humus. Humus provides channels in soil for air and water, and humic acid makes it easier for plants to pick up nutrients. Properly managed [grasslands] can sequester substantial amounts of carbon, binding it up in soil and making a cow's pasture "a carbon sink"*.'[8]

But soil is not only good for carbon sequestering, but also for our own health, through 'soil-borne wellness'. Research is discovering that having a connection with soil – through growing food, gardening or other soil based activities – can be better for health and wellbeing than just the benefits of the produce or the activity itself.[9] Introducing soils through internal planting, green walls and roofs and urban agriculture within buildings, and by getting people active in maintaining them, can help provide healthy buildings that both maintain and improve the health of occupants.

PERSPECTIVE
LANDSCAPE ARCHITECTURE AND SUSTAINABILITY
CLAIRE THIRLWALL,
THIRLWALL ASSOCIATES

You design your buildings to use minimal energy using sustainable materials. What if the surrounding site could sequester carbon, improve air quality and help reduce the risk of flooding?

Well-designed landscapes provide a more attractive environment to live and work in, including habitat creation, designing accessible circulation routes and screening intrusive structures. Yet there are lesser-known benefits that could be gained through careful landscape design.

Landscape schemes have environmental impacts. Plants raised in greenhouses and transported to site have a high carbon footprint, and unsustainable materials like peat are still commonly used. However the landscape sector has the ability to work in a far more sustainable way and even to mitigate some of the environmental impacts of construction projects.

Carbon sequestration is normally associated with forests or peat bogs. However, work by seed suppliers has shown that, given the right conditions, grass areas can perform as well as or even better than forests at carbon sequestration. It is difficult to estimate the total amount of green space in England, however 40% of the land in the UK is managed as pasture and semi-natural grassland, compared to just under 12% that is covered by woodlands. If all these grassland areas were managed for carbon sequestration the impact could be substantial.

Other potential benefits can include designing planting schemes for maximum benefit to pollinating species – this is important as the number of bee species has fallen in many parts of the UK – and using blocks of tree planting to reduce the energy use of a building by creating shade in the summer and reducing the impact of cooling winds in the winter. In addition, links can be created between dispersed areas of habitat by planting wildlife corridors and providing areas for urban food production.

There are many reasons to implement a well-designed landscape scheme and the benefits can be significant. However it is important not to rely solely on practical benefits to justify a landscape scheme as some sites are so constrained few features can be incorporated. The primary aim should be to design an attractive landscape. Beauty is a reason in itself.

Restorative Demonstrators

The LEED Platinum Leopold Center in Winsconsin,[10] which demonstrates Leopold's Land Ethics, achieved a LEED score of 61/69 – more than any other building in the US at that time. It was the first carbon-neutral building certified by LEED in 2015, with annual operations accounting for no net gain in carbon dioxide emissions. It is a net zero energy building, meeting all of its energy needs on site, using 70% less energy than code, and the Center's roof-mounted solar array is projected to meet 110% of the building's energy needs on an annual basis.

The concept of habitat exchange should extend beyond merely those projects pursuing LBC recognition, and be seen as a key net-positive or offsetting initiative. Sustainable development is broader than just any one project: it extends to wider sustainable protection of our wilderness and **peatlands areas** that have a restorative function in respect of carbon and water.

The UK peatlands,[11] predominantly made up of sphagnum moss, account for about 10% of the UK's land area. It is estimated peatlands store about three billion tonnes of carbon, more than 20 times the volume stored by UK forests. The peatlands store more carbon below ground than plants do above ground. Consequently, sphagnum moss is now seen as a vital weapon in the war against climate change.

Figure 4.2 Sphagnum moss, peatland, Scottish Highlands

Unfortunately UK peatlands are in a bad state of health, but they can be restored relatively cheaply and easily. Once the dominant vegetation, sphagnum moss, is returned, peatlands quickly begin absorbing carbon once again. A healthy bog also functions as an excellent water filter – an important aspect of sustainable water programmes, since 75% of our water catchment is in peatland areas.

Lancashire Wildlife Trust's natural carbon capture scheme provides opportunity for offsetting built environment carbon while making a positive contribution to Peatlands habitat restoration.[12]

Scotsman John Muir, an influential thinker and writer on wilderness issues and land ecology, was founder of US National Parks and the environmentally influential Sierra Club. In the UK, the **John Muir Trust** was established in the UK in 1983 to promote wild places as essential for both people and wildlife, with a mission to conserve and protect wild places with indigenous animals, plants and soils for the benefit of present and future generations.[13] Organisations like the John Muir Trust could provide an excellent opportunity for exploring and promoting habitat exchange for the built environment. Imagine the area of land that could be set aside from every new build serious about restorative sustainability.

AIR

The air quality app on my phone provides me with alarming statistics on the number of deaths resulting from poor air quality in UK cities, per hour, per day, and the level of air quality above that recommended by the World Health Organisation (WHO).

The visibility and health impact of air quality in cities such as London and Beijing is well documented. Within the first week of 2016, London had exceeded the EU annual target for days above the safe health limit.

Air quality in buildings, where we spend up to 90% of our time, has a huge influence on our wellbeing, health and comfort, and is recognised as the key factor in sick building syndrome. Unsurprisingly, then, the quality of air in buildings also has a major influence on productivity, learning and creativity. Health and business costs relating to the consequences of poor air quality is huge.

Air quality is determined by:

- **the level of pollutants present within the building fabric and materials**
- **the operation of the building**
- **pollutants from external air**
- **user activities.**

The WELL Building Standard and the Living Building Challenge focus heavily on air quality. They seek not only to reduce the impact of poor air quality but to improve air quality such that it contributes to the improved health, comfort, wellbeing and productivity of building occupants.

Approaches to date have focused on reducing the impact of poor air quality by tackling the source of pollutants, improving air ventilation, and the introduction of biophilic thinking, recognising the benefits of nature in improving air-related health quality. Yet it remains shortsighted, costly and irresponsible to continue using designs, systems and materials with known health issues, only to later attempt to reduce the impact through building in operation measures.

With a challenge to the built environment to tackle air quality – not just to reduce impact, but to improve the health of building users – a holistic and collaborative view of buildings is required, one involving not just professionals from across the built environment but also what we currently see as unconventional collaborations with health practitioners, air quality researchers and related charity groups.

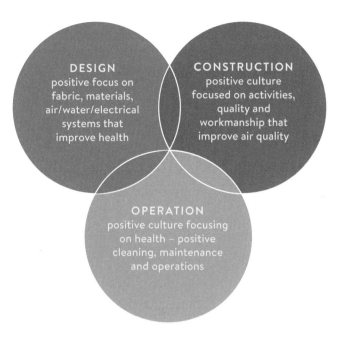

Figure 4.3 Improving health: net-positive air quality

Every Breath We Take

The 2016 *Every Breath We Take* report from the Royal College of Physicians is a sobering update on the human and cost consequences of poor air quality.[14] It focuses not only on outdoor air quality, notoriously poor within many of our cities, but also on the consequences arising from poor indoor air quality, significantly triggered through the design, construction and operation of the buildings we live, work and play in.

> 'Each year in the UK, around 40,000 deaths are attributable to exposure to outdoor air pollution, with more linked also to exposure to indoor pollutants.'
>
> EVERY BREATH WE TAKE

The report estimates that the cost to society, business and health services in the UK adds up to more than £20 billion every year. This is a prime example of how, in the built environment, we externalise the real cost of low cost construction.

The report focuses on pollutants from buildings that occur during operation, but also addresses air quality arising from pollutants during the construction phase, namely '*the high volume of construction transport, predominantly diesel, in addition to the pollutants known to be asthmatics, organic and mineral dust, or carcinogenic material (asbestos fibres in older buildings, and formaldehyde and VOCs in newer builds.)*'

The built environment is responsible for an increasingly complex cocktail of air quality issues. And the report warns that, without better understanding and monitoring of air quality during construction and occupancy, new technologies, the use of advanced materials and approaches such as 3D printing could lead to 'novel inhaled hazards and risks'.

Every Breath We Take makes a number of recommendations:

- **Lead by example in the NHS:** **to design, build and maintain health facilities that are net-health-positive.**

- **Quantify the relationship between indoor air pollution and health:** **Pressure for ever more energy efficient buildings with lower carbon footprints raises the potential of reducing air quality in homes, offices and schools. A holistic and collaborative effort is required across built environment organisations, and research and health organisations to develop policies and standards.**

According to the findings of the *Every Breath We Take* report, there really should be no air quality performance gap, as even a small gap will result in human health issues and externalised health costs.

In line with the increasingly popular Living Building Challenge and WELL Build Standard, air quality must become a key element of performance gap analysis. The design stage sets the required air quality threshold that is assessed post-construction, over a 12-month period of full occupation, and then on a regular ongoing basis. Established standards such as BREEAM and LEED should base awards of certification on *proven* air quality.

This is a CSR (corporate social responsibility) issue of high magnitude for those who commission buildings, those who design and construct, and those who manage buildings. A responsible built environment sector cannot accept anything less.

PERSPECTIVE
AIR POLLUTION
CLAIRE THIRLWALL,
THIRLWALL ASSOCIATES

Air pollution is a major risk to health, with the World Health Organisation (WHO) estimating that urban pollution causes 1.3 million deaths per year worldwide. Trees within landscape schemes can reduce the impact of pollution in two ways: they absorb pollutants, trapping the molecules within their leaves, and they trap and retain particulates such as dust and smoke on the surfaces of their leaves and branches. A London study estimated that trees remove 2,100 tonnes of pollutants in the Greater London Authority area each year. The size and species of tree is important: species such as lime and beech are more effective at removing particles, so the correct specification is vital.

Restorative Demonstrators

Buildings can *improve* air quality through biophilic designs, biomimicry and material or technological innovations that remove harmful particles from the air. An increasingly common approach is the inclusion of indoor living green walls, and when incorporated into schools add an air quality educational aspect to the function of removing VOCs and pollutants from the air.

As Barbara Jones comments in Chapter 5, healthy indoor air quality can be maintained, even improved, by replacing cement with lime-based renders.

With construction projects notoriously dusty environments, incorporating living walls as project hoardings – as used, for example, on the **Library of Birmingham** during construction[15] – can reduce dust, improve air quality, and demonstrate the responsible construction approach from the contractor and project team.

More radical and technical solutions are seen in the **Smog Free Tower** by Studio Roosegaarde, initially installed in Rotterdam, designed to remove smog-causing particles from city air.[16] The tower '*uses ion technology to create smog-free bubbles of public space, allowing people to breathe and experience clean air for free.*'

We are familiar with the biophilic health and air quality benefits of living walls within new builds. Incorporating living walls as construction project site hoarding can also provide healthy working places and address the construction impact on air quality within the local community.

Figure 4.4 A green living wall as a construction site hoarding, Central London

LIGHT

Light is Medicine
Speaking at the WOBI (World of Business Ideas) World Business Forum in 2015, Dellos and Well Being Standard CEO Paul Scialla described light as *potential medicine*', and noted how artificial light from the built environment has, over a considerable period, negatively impacted on human health, changing sleep patterns and productivity. This impact can be reset, in both existing buildings and in new buildings, with innovations such as circadian lighting.

Circadian Lighting
The circadian rhythm is our inbuilt clock, aligned to daily natural cycles, that 'regulates' behaviour and health. We subconsciously perceive the position of the sun, the changing colour and spectrum of light during a 24-hour cycle. This provides triggers for behaviour, sleep, resting, eating, attentiveness, relaxation and more.

Disruption to our circadian rhythm through lack of exposure to natural light cycles is now linked to a number of health issues relating to sleep, eating, bipolar and metabolic disorders. In addition, urban lighting and night light pollution removes the connection to natural light cycles, and has been likened to being in a mini 'jetlag' state.

Responsible organisations within the built environment, whether as building owners, operators, designers or constructors, need to explore, understand and address the lighting impact of buildings on people, including the task lighting provided for construction activities.

Restorative Demonstration
The BREEAM Excellent **Dyson Centre for Neonatal Care** at RUH Bath, a low-carbon unit constructed from cross laminated timber, boasts a good number of sustainability features. The *Dezeen* case study in 2011 described the project as a '*pioneering holistic and therapeutic approach*' that allows staff to practise new methods of care for premature and sick babies.[17]

Focus on lighting, both natural and artificial, recognises the importance of circadian rhythms at neonatal stages of life, with areas light-controlled to ensure babies gain awareness of changing light through the day and night. And importantly, the wellbeing of parents and staff is addressed as they can also experience changing external conditions through lighting, window seating areas, skylights and access to green courtyard spaces.

Figure 4.5 The Dyson Centre for Neonatal Care, RUH Bath

1 Efforts to address climate change have hinged on the legally binding agreement aiming to hold global temperatures to 2°C above pre-industrial levels. The 2015 Paris Agreement included the intent to target a global 1.5°C temperature cap alongside the 2°C goal.

2 Benyus, J., *Biomimicry, Innovation Inspired by Nature*, 1998.

3 Palwyn, M., *Biomimicry in Architecture*, 2011.

4 Monbiot, G., *Feral*, ISBN 9780226205694, 2014.

5 Cambridge University https://www.dropbox.com/s/wdozqlye9qfyvix/Lamb_Main_Text_NCLIM-14111643B%20(2).pdf?dl=0* See also http://www.farming.co.uk/news/article/12020

6 http://www.theguardian.com/artanddesign/2011/may/01/brockholes-preston-review-rowan-moore

7 Leopold, A., *A Sand County Almanac*, ISBN: 9780195007770, 1949.

8 Hayes, D., *Cowed*, W. W. Norton & Company, ISBN 0393239942, 2015.

9 http://www.healinglandscapes.org/blog/2011/01/its-in-the-dirt-bacteria-in-soil-makes-us-happier-smarter/

10 Leopold Center in Winsconsin: http://www.aldoleopold.org/Visit/leopoldcenter.shtml

11 UK Peatlands project: http://www.iucn-uk-peatlandprogramme.org/

12 http://www.lancswt.org.uk/how-you-can-help/business/natural-carbon-capture

13 https://www.johnmuirtrust.org

14 https://www.rcplondon.ac.uk/projects/outputs/every-breath-we-take-lifelong-impact-air-pollution

15 http://www.urbangreening.info/#!birmingham-library-green-wall/c15ew

16 https://www.studioroosegaarde.net/project/smog-free-project/info

17 Dyson Centre for Neonatal Intensive Care Unit: http://www.dezeen.com/2011/08/08/the-dyson-centre-for-neonatal-care-by-feilden-clegg-bradley-studios/

CHAPTER FIVE

RESTORATIVE APPROACHES 2
ENERGY, WATER, MATERIALS, WASTE AND CARBON

ENERGY · WATER · MATERIALS · WASTE · CARBON

Figure 5.1

ENERGY

This chapter continues the exploration of innovations, inspirations and challenges for rethinking construction for the ecological age, enabling restorative and net positive futures.

> 'The road to energy independence, economic recovery and greenhouse gas reductions runs through the building sector.'

EDWARD MAZRIA[1]

The built environment sector, responsible for using 40% of our energy, has a huge influence on energy sourcing issues. If we continue to design and build buildings to be solely dependent on fossil fuel energy, we maintain the demand for dirty fuels such as coal, tar sands and fracking, and are part-responsible for their attendant problems. The stress on divided communities in Lancashire in the summer of 2015 as fracking permissions were debated and denied is only part of the problems of '*dirty*' fuels. The environmental and health related issues are well documented elsewhere, but the built environment's responsibility less so.

If the built environment sector was to design new buildings and renovate old ones based on renewables, we would flip demand away from fossil fuels to renewables, from dirty to clean energy, from less bad to more good. This has been the principal argument of Edward Mazria at Architecture 2030 for many years.

In *Third Industrial Revolution, How Lateral Power is Transforming the Economy and the World*, Jeremy Rifkin describes the fossil fuel energy market as a sunset economy, one in irreversible decline.[2] He sees buildings as instrumental in bringing about the next industrial revolution, driven by the convergence of innovation in communications, energy and transportation.

A question for the built environment sector – the same question that Rifkin asks of other industries – is whether we want to be part of the '*sunset fossil fuel economy*' or to move forward to be part of the emerging renewables economy. And it may well be a question of survival. Rifkin's future vision of the is one that is already emerging; if it is not driven by those within the sector, it will be driven by others, potentially major disruption to the built environment.

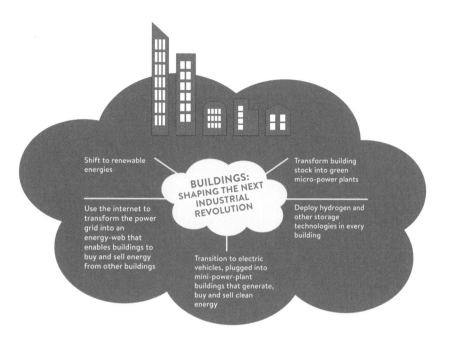

Figure 5.2 Buildings shaping the next industrial revolution

Most, if not all, countries have targets for energy efficiency (as demonstrated in Table 5.1). There are, however, a number of factors to consider with these targets. Firstly, while they are seeking only to reduce carbon emissions from energy use through being less bad, it is encouraging to see net-positive and zero fossil fuel targets feature in a number of countries' ambitions, namely France, Germany and South Korea.

Net-Positive Energy

It is a requirement of the Living Building Challenge that buildings rely solely on renewable forms of energy and operate year-round in a safe, pollution-free manner. Additionally, 105% of the project's energy needs must be supplied by on-site renewable energy on a net annual basis, without the use of on-site combustion. Projects must provide on-site energy storage for resiliency. Evidence of compliance with design criteria and demonstrating a net-positive energy performance over a 12-month seasonal period is required prior to certification.

As the Bullitt Center has demonstrated, it is absolutely essential to fully explore and understand building energy loads, individual thermal comfort issues, occupant behaviour and the management of energy usage in building operations in order to balance energy supply and demand.

To talk of outperforming others as if in some competition is unfair to the ethos of the Bullitt Center,[3] given that the buildings goal is driving change in the marketplace faster and further, looking to replicate the project *'a thousand-fold, a million-fold and fast'*.

Beyond Net-Positive Buildings

There is an interesting debate as to how we should approach existing public or domestic buildings of value that are not energy efficient, and those it would not be practical or economically viable to renovate to acceptable energy performance standards.

We need to cease seeing buildings as individual entities, as energy end-of-line energy-user and energy-wasting nodes, but as an interconnected grid. Net-positive buildings, connected to micro and nano grids, can support underperforming buildings that we wish to keep for significant cultural, historic or social value.

Energy net-positive building performance can be extended over a community rather than individual buildings. As we have more energy net-positive buildings (Germany has already renovated over two million buildings to become mini power plants, connected to a power grid), this community approach becomes more and more viable, and good reason to build net-positive requirements into planning, sustainability standards and building regulations.

PERSPECTIVE
DO BUILDINGS WORK?
SOFIE PELSMAKERS,
ENVIRONMENTAL ARCHITECT

In designing and building buildings we never ask ourselves, or those using them, if they 'work'. In the last few years, we have come to realise that often our buildings don't work, especially from technical and energy perspectives. Typically, occupants are never involved in the design or specification of a building, yet they are often held responsible for any (mal)functioning. This is a displacement of where the responsibility of design lies: if occupants are not asked if and how they want to use the space or systems, or if what was designed would suit their day-to-day lives and patterns, are they really responsible for a building's performance?

Additionally, building performance will become harder to predict as we design more and more complex buildings to not only provide shelter, but also take into account a changing climate and incorporate new efficient technologies, products and materials alongside buildings incorporating local energy generation; much more can go wrong during building and commissioning, for example. We have recognised the benefit of collaboration with other consultants and often the contractor to deliver these complex buildings, but we have unfortunately stuck to limited collaboration (often to the exclusion of the client and users). This must change: the actual building is unlikely to perform as predicted when user occupancy and building use expectations are excluded from models.

The industry is slowly starting to realise that this added complexity in building design and construction cannot be met by business-as-usual design and procurement processes. Finally, we are starting to see the value in going back to check whether the building performs in terms of energy use and CO_2 emissions, and whether it meets occupant thermal comfort and satisfaction. While post-occupancy and building performance evaluations are still not standard on each project (when they should be), putting people centre-stage in our design process is long overdue and is often even neglected in low-energy buildings.

The environmental impact of our designs should not exclude the impact of design on occupants. For instance, we might consider embodied energy, but what is the impact of the specified materials on occupant health? We consider a building's energy demand – but are the stipulated daylighting, noise or ventilation levels sufficient from a human-health perspective? While we consider building overheating in summer (or in a changing climate), are we sure this is based on realistic occupancy behaviour and does not require people to operate blinds or open and close windows when they cannot do so? And how do building security, access to outdoor space and local amenities alongside maintenance regimes (directly arising from material specification) affect occupant happiness and sense of place?

Buildings should allow occupants to interact with, change and affect the building design, so it can be modified to meet changing needs and uses over time. To truly build sustainably, we need to marry low-energy building with healthy, adaptable and resilient buildings. Failure to do so means there is a danger that we tackle the building energy balance to the detriment of a more humane architecture. The two are not mutually exclusive.

Restorative Demonstrator: The Bullitt Center
Brad Kahn, Bullitt Center Foundation[4]

In the 12-month period ending 15 December, 2015, the Bullitt Center had an EUI (Energy Use Intensity)[5] of 10.1 kBTU/gsf . Needless to say, we are pleased with the way the building is operating, particularly as, in the US, EUI includes tenant loads. During this period the building was fully leased but staffing is rising at a number of the tenant organisations so we would expect EUI to rise a bit over time. It is worth noting the Bullitt Center is an all electric building.

During the same time period, our solar array produced 54% more electricity than we used. We were net-positive for eight months of the year, with only four months that we drew net energy off the grid. Of course, we were hugely net-positive for the whole 12-month period.

For comparison, we typically use the following generic reference points:

- ■ **EUI for all office buildings in Seattle: 90**
- ■ **EUI for office buildings built to Seattle's new (2009) code: 50**
- ■ **EUI for LEED Platinum office buildings that get all the energy credits: 32**
- ■ **Maximum Bullitt Centre EUI, supported by electricity from the solar array: 16**
- ■ **Actual EUI for the Bullitt Center, 15 December 2014 to 15 December 2015: 10.1**

Put differently, the average new office building in Seattle, built to an energy code that is widely claimed to be among the toughest in the US, uses approximately five times the energy per square foot that we do.

'The Bullitt Center is about opening a wedge into the future. Once something exists, no one can say it's impossible.' Denis Hayes

Perhaps the best known of Living Building Challenge projects, the Bullitt Center in Seattle, designed for a building life of 250 years, achieved Living Building Certification in 2015. The building demonstrates an impressive array of net-positive and biophilic features, earning the project the accolade of the world's greenest commercial building.

Figure 5.3 Bullitt Center, Seattle

WATER

Water is Life

We have an increasing pressure on water resources as a result of population increase, economic growth and development, climate change, pollution, flooding and other challenges. Water quality impacts on our health, wellbeing and economic development. And the built environment is a major influencer as both a problem and an enabler of restorative water solutions. Buildings significantly impact on water use and wastage, managing water availability, dealing with blackwater, using greywater and innovating with water-free approaches, dealing with and harnessing rain and storm water.

Positively, a building can act as a water purifier, in cases only using the water that falls on it within a closed loop, net-positive water system, and cleansing what it doesn't use, in the same way that a tree returns 80% of the water it harvests through its leaves to other plants and species. Once we see buildings as part of this ecosystem, with their own closed-loop water system, connected and restorative, the burden on both water supply and water discharge can be significantly reduced.

Beyond SUDS

Sustainable Urban Drainage Systems is the UK expression for the collection of measures for managing surface water, associated flooding and pollution issues within urban areas. Examples of SUDS include green roof soakaways, swales, infiltration trenches, ponds and wetlands. Ideally SUDS provides a natural water management solution in urban areas where natural capability is not available, or has been removed through changes to ground surfaces, increased hard impermeable surfaces, paved gardens and the like.

Flooding

Flooding will be the most visible and damaging consequence of climate change in the UK. Floods in the south-west of the UK in 2012 and in the north in 2015–16 have been recognised as a consequence of climate change. Yet while climate change is causing the increased rainfall, it is human influence on the environment that is causing both the frequency and magnitude of flooding. Increased hard surfaces within towns, cities and gardens have overwhelmed and caused failure within our existing systems. Our flood defence infrastructures, agriculture and land management approaches have been designed to fight and control nature rather than to understand and work with it.

What has become evident is that these existing systems, many based on SUDS thinking, cannot cope with increased rainfall. The answer lies not in increased *defence*, but more natural approaches. Environmentalist and proponents of rewilding advocate for a flood defence and management strategy that is sympathetic with nature. This restorative approach to flood management proposes increased planting of trees (woodland can absorb 60% more floodwater than pasture land), better land management (peat restoration, preventing damage through heathland burning practices), established flood plain, and allowing natural river courses to deal with flash floods.

Water as Biophilic Enabler

Water features within the *Terrapin Bright Green 14 Patterns of Biophilic Design*,[7] reinforcing occupant link with place and nature. Research as noted within *14 Patterns* indicates that incorporating water into building design can also:

- **reduce stress, increase feelings of tranquility, lower heart rate and blood pressure**
- **improve concentration and memory restoration**
- **enhance perception**
- **lead to positive emotional responses.**

Restorative Demonstrators

CIRS, the Centre for Interactive Research on Sustainability at the University of British Columbia, was first conceived in 1999 by Dr John Robinson, a professor at UBC, as an opportunity to push the envelope of sustainable design by integrating passive design strategies with the most advanced sustainable technologies of the time to achieve an off-the-chart level of performance. It has achieved LEED Platinum and Living Building Challenge Petal certifications.

100% of all reclaimed water used at CIRS originates from the building and the campus sewer system; it is treated on site and reused within the building. The solar aquatic system, an ecologically engineered system based on processes existing in nature, consumes human biological waste to produce clean water.[8]

Addressing the Living Building Challenge goal to harvest and purify rainwater to satisfy all the water needs of the building's occupants, and to cleanse and return used water to the hydrological cycle in an undiminished condition, **the Bullitt Center, Seattle,** has an impressive approach to its net-zero water status.

The most significant feature (and the one most popular on site tours) is an array of water-free composting toilets. Up to 75% of the annual rainwater that lands on the building is collected and stored in a 50,000-gallon tank in the basement. This ensures the building can maintain its water needs for considerable periods without rainfall or through periods of drought. Water from the tank is treated and used for non-potable uses and, when permits allow, for potable water.

Greywater from the building goes through filter screens to a 400-gallon storage tank in the basement. From here it is pumped to 'constructed wetlands' located on the roof over a portion of the second level.

Waste from the foam flushing toilets and urinals drops to ten composting units within the basement where heat treatment ensures pathogens and contaminants are sterilised. Annually, the units produce over 100 ft³ of compost, which is mixed locally with other composted material and used as a soil improver.

Figure 5.4 CIRS Building, UBC, Vancouver

MATERIALS

'The materials we build with can affect our wellbeing as much as the food we eat, the water we drink and the air we breathe.'

HEALTHY BUILDING NETWORK[9]

Healthy or Toxic?

Historically we have only had a few hundred building products to use in construction – products that were generally local, chemical free and natural. With the development of chemical innovation we now have millions of products, which are now mostly non-local and have non-natural elements.

The *Domestic Chemical Cocktail* paper published by the Gaia Group illustrates not only the health impact, but also the lack of sector and public awareness of healthy materials in construction.[10] It states that of the '*55,000 materials available to the building industry, only 3% have been tested for their toxicity on humans, and … there is compelling evidence that toxicity in a very large number of ubiquitous building materials is a contributory trigger to people with asthma and allergies.*'

As the paper points out, the construction sector has moved significantly in good practice for health and safety on construction process – yet we are still a long way from establishing toxicity as a buildings-in-use concern. This is despite evidence to indicate that many construction materials present a potential health hazard to occupants and to the environment.

We should however reflect on the construction site approach to COSHH (Control of Substances Hazardous to Health) and question just why we continue to use materials '*hazardous to health*' (even under tight control of protective equipment, correct ventilation and storage) when more benign materials are available.
It also throws an interesting light on those organisations that have adopted a '*Do no harm*' policy, only to continue to allow and to incorporate materials into their constructions that evidence shows have the potential to harm during manufacture, installation or in use.

Red List

The Red List is the Living Building Challenge (LBC) compendium of building materials that present the greatest impact to human and ecosystem health. The intent of the Red List is to eliminate these materials from construction and from buildings, replacing them with healthy, non-toxic alternatives.

LIVING BUILDING CHALLENGE RED LIST OF MATERIALS AND CHEMICALS

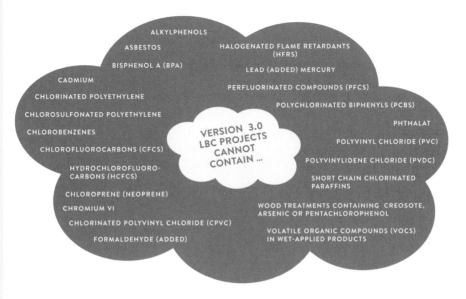

Figure 5.5 Living Building Challenge Red List of materials and chemicals

There are a few exceptions to the use of some of these chemicals, as detailed in the LBC materials handbook, but each exception requires evidence of seeking alternatives and of advocating for change with the manufacturer of Red List non-compliant material.

There are other lists of note with the same ethos as the Red List, such as the Pharos Project[11] and Perkins+Will 'Transparency'.[12] All embrace precautionary principle thinking – meaning that in the absence of other evidence, the burden of proof that a material is not harmful falls on those specifying.

Many will be familiar with the Montreal Protocol list created to prohibit the use of CFCs (ozone depleting substances). Over time other substances have been added to the list, and it is currently under review.[13] It has been heralded a huge success, proving it is possible to remove harmful substances from use. However, an inadvertent consequence of the removal of CFCs has been an increase in its replacement – HCFCs (hydrochlorofluorocarbons) – themselves now considered an equally harmful and carcinogenic risk.

The Material Schedule developed by British Land in the UK, embedded within their Sustainability Brief for Developments and applied to all of their major projects, is a prime example of clients taking a lead on managing material impact.[14] The Material Schedule not only prohibits or restricts materials that present health or ecological hazards, but emphasises its requirement for standards such as Timber FSC or PEFC and encourages standards such as Grown in Britain.

Only once we fully understand the impact and nature of construction materials that we use today can we make real progress on ecological and environmental restorative sustainability.

Other material certification schemes seeking to ensure that environmentally or socially unacceptable materials and processes are ideally removed from use or strictly controlled are detailed in Table 5.2 at the end of this chapter.

The Circular Economy

The Ellen MacArthur Foundation, the leading champion of circular economy, describes our current 'linear' approach as 'take + make + dispose', based on large quantities of cheap, available resources.[15] As resources become unavailable, inaccessible or simply too costly, however, this linear approach, dominant since the Industrial Revolution, is starting to creak.

As an alternative, the circular economy defined by the Ellen MacArthur Foundation is restorative, it seeks to maintain products, components and materials at their highest value at all times. Using both a technical and a biological cycle, the model describes products designed to enable cycles of disassembly and reuse, thereby reducing, delaying or eliminating waste. The result is to avoid down-cycling, conversion to energy or disposal to landfill.

Research carried out by Imperial College London on behalf of waste management organisation Veolia estimates the circular economy to be valued at £29bn per annum and predicts it will create some 117,000 new jobs in the UK economy.[16] It is difficult to estimate what proportion of this value could be built environment related, but given the sector's 40% rule of thumb waste impact, it could be highly significant.

Applying circular economy thinking to buildings has been slow and a challenge. How can we scale up the incorporation of previously used materials and components into buildings and then ensure they are available for reuse at the end of the building's life? There are, however, examples that demonstrate the potential, such as a new office project in Duiven, near Arnhem in the Netherlands. Here 80% of materials used have been sourced from existing buildings, and 80% of materials in the new building will be available for reuse at the end of the building's lifespan.

It is a Living Building Challenge requirement to include at least one salvaged material per 500m^2 of gross building area, or for the building to be an adaptive reuse of an existing structure. In addition, projects must implement a Material Conservation Management Plan that explains how the project 'optimises materials throughout the design, construction, operation and end of life phases of a building'.

Material Passports

'Waste is material without data. Once we add data to material we (re)create its value and prevent waste.'[17]

The concept of the Material Passport, which details life histories and potentials for reuse, is key to the circular economy approach of reusing products, components or materials from building to building.

Douglas Mulhall, Academic Chair of 'Cradle to Cradle for Innovation and Quality' at the Rotterdam School of Management, describes Material Passports as adding a new dimension to material quality. They detail materials' suitability for recovery and reuse in other products or buildings, enabling buildings to become 'resource repleters not resource depleters'.[18] Materials passports must become the restorative sustainability version of (new) Product Data Sheets within Building Information Management (BIM) libraries and models.

The Dutch development organisation Delta Developments, which has embraced cradle to cradle thinking, is among the leading organisations now seeing buildings as 'material farms to be harvested' for future projects, such as the Schiphol Trade Park Development, a circular economy concept with ambitions to become the most sustainable business park in Europe.

Design for Deconstruction
Key to macro circular economy thinking – and the capacity to recycle whole buildings and major components as well as materials – is a design ethos that allows for disassembly. In Design for Disassembly in the Built Environment: A Guide to Closed-Loop Design and Building, authors Brad Guy and Nicholas Ciarimboli outline a forward thinking set of 10 Principles for Design for Disassembly.[19]

Postmodern Methods of Construction
Modern Methods of Construction (MMC), a term in use over the last two decades that describes off-site and modular, volumetric construction, is perhaps now a dated title for what is becoming more commonplace and should perhaps be labelled Postmodern Methods of Construction, recognising the broader inclusion of such emerging techniques as 3d printing, nano technology, and embedded robotics to automate building reconfiguration.

Modular construction and off-site assembly approach is increasing being seen as a viable solution to addressing time, quality and performance issues of homes, schools and offices.

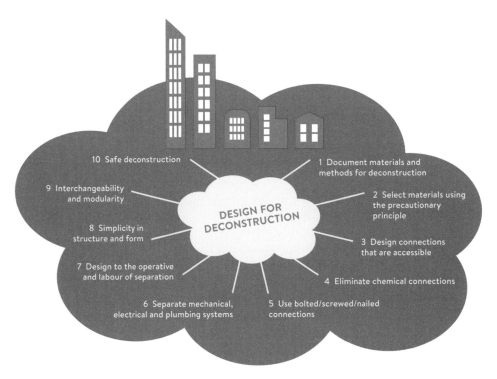

Figure 5.6 Design for deconstruction

The BREEAM Outstanding Bright Building RE:CENTRE, on the University of Bradford campus, demonstrates the ethos of the circular economy, incorporating many of the Design for Disassembly principles. It also includes a number of restorative sustainability approaches, such air quality control through natural ventilation and the use of natural materials such as the hemp concrete and timber that have been used as the main structure.

Figure 5.7 RE:CENTRE, University of Bradford

MMC CURRENT BENEFITS AND OPPORTUNITIES	MMC DISADVANTAGES AND BARRIERS
Factory control QA	Scaling of negative design impacts
Lower production costs	Entrenchment of practice
Reduced waste (any waste is generated off site, where there is greater chance of reusing)	Location of established plants
Embracing BIM	Access and large heavy load transportation issues
Safety	Engineered products installed by unskilled operatives
Factory relationship rather than construction relationship	
Reduced number of construction miles	
Better working conditions	
Improved standardisation	
Repeatable supply chain	
Embracing restorative sustainability	
Net-positive energy and water production	
Healthy materials	
Understanding the ecological and social handprint of an organisation	
JUST/DECLARE/Living Product Challenge	

The off-site sector is now in a prime position to move forward and champion restorative or regenerative sustainability thinking, seeking, for example, DECLARE or Living Product Challenge recognition for their products or production process. This sector of the building environment arguably has greater influence on net-positive water and energy, health and happiness, through, for example, replacing toxic chemicals with safe, natural adhesives and insulation and through embracing localism movements (such as Grown in Britain), than a traditional on-site production process would ever have. In addition, to attain JUST recognition the off-site sector need not follow mainstream construction sector issues when it comes to diversity and equity, but understand and address the ecological and social handprint of its operations.

PERSPECTIVE
HEALTHY, NOT 'LESS HARMFUL'
ALEX WHITCROFT,
ASSOCIATE DIRECTOR, BERE ARCHITECTS

It is an astounding period to look back on: carcinogenic heavy metals routinely added to building materials; lead in contact with skin and drinking water; phthalates and BPA in plastics and resins in contact with food and water; nerve- and organ-disrupting VOCs in virtually every wet finish.[20] The ignorant days of the mid-20th century, we might think; the era of DDT and asbestos, leaded petrol and supposedly no health risks from cigarettes. But it's not last century – it's now.

When we buy something like a loaf of bread we don't expect it to contain toxins. And we expect to see ingredients. In fact, that's the law. With buildings it's different. Most of us spend most of our lives in buildings. We breathe the air within them; we prepare our food in them and from the water that runs through them. And yet, in the vast majority of cases, their constituents and provenance are completely unknown.

Not only is there not the same level of mandated transparency as in many other sectors, but the construction industry largely does not consider such information consumer facing – and so building users and the public remain disconnected and uninformed, and therefore cannot demand change. In the meantime we continue to use myriad harmful chemicals as we erect the buildings that will house us and our children for the next X decades. We, construction industry professionals, are complicit in this. I had a conversation with an architect recently about a product that I was disappointed to find had no Material Safety Data Sheet (MSDS). They replied, '*What is an MSDS sheet?*' As industry professionals we wouldn't try to argue, '*Well, I just hadn't really read up on health and safety developments for the last 20 years,*' or, '*Why would I have checked if that product was fire-resistant before specifying it in a fire escape?*' So how come we are doing it with material health?

The human and environmental toxicity of DDT was discovered in the early 1940s, but it took 30 years for it to be banned. Dr Montague Murray wrote on the health effects of asbestos in 1899; the first documented death came in 1906.[21] Yet it wasn't until 1999 that the UK implemented a full ban on the substance.[22] That's around a century later. Worse yet, due to industry lobbying, asbestos is still not fully banned in the US[23] – and it still kills over 100,000 people around the world annually.[24] All too often, we still take an '*innocent until proven guilty*' approach to material toxicity.

Even once a problem is identified, we then take a passive approach to catalysing reform. Here is a good example: the chloride monomer in PVC is a known carcinogen. PVC itself is a persistent/accumulative pollutant, and often contains other toxic substances such as cadmium, lead and phthalates. Both its manufacture and disposal can generate nerve- and immune-damaging dioxins. But PVC isn't banned. It's still used in a huge range of building products, including water system components, electronics, gaskets and more. Not only that, I see PVC products touted by manufacturers as 'green' or 'sustainable'. Working on a Living Building Challenge project a few years ago I found myself on the phone to a manufacturer, trying to find non-toxic (Red List-free) products – and being told that they only made the part I was after in PVC. Yet to my surprise they added, 'We hate the stuff: it's toxic as hell and so corrosive it destroys our moulds faster than any other plastic.' The manufacturer went on to say it would probably even be cheaper to make non-PVC components, given the tooling savings, but the trouble was the economies of scale as everyone simply specified and bought the PVC product.

By and large, this isn't a technological problem. It's a behavioural one. As designers and specifiers we need to start educating ourselves, asking more questions about the health and environmental impacts of the design choices we make in sourcing, manufacture, use and disposal. As clients we need to demand healthy buildings and start holding professionals to account for failing to design responsibly.

We need stronger sustainable construction regulations and targets (rather than their continual rolling back and weakening by national policymakers). We must demand the prohibition of known toxins in materials and lobby for more transparency in the ingredients of building products (between manufacturers and specifiers, but also to the public). We need to stop designing without consideration for the environmental impacts of sourcing and manufacture, or still behaving as if there is an 'away', where all our solely down-cyclable and/or toxic construction waste can harmlessly go. (The construction industry produces more waste, globally, than any other industry.)[25] And, I would argue, we need to advocate for legislation on terminology in advertising such as 'sustainable', 'healthy' or 'biodegradable'.

In the words of Martin Luther King Jr, 'We are now faced with the fact that tomorrow is today ... Over the bleached bones and jumbled residue of numerous civilisations are written the pathetic words: "Too late".'[26] Let us not be too late. Again.

PERSPECTIVE
WHY CEMENT SHOULD NEVER BE USED WITH NATURAL BUILDINGS
BARBARA JONES,
STRAW WORKS

Although I am often asked to help with other people's designs, one of my principles is never to design with cement. One of the major issues with cement is that the problems it causes are not visible or apparent straight away. In fact, they can take many years to become obvious.

As I began to learn about natural materials in the 1990s, as well as 'straw-bale building' I studied lime and clay plasters and cob building. I also had an interest in old houses, and I realised that all our old houses (built before 1900) are built entirely of natural materials – in fact, so too are all old houses everywhere around the world.

A major problem with cement and concrete is that it attracts or 'wicks' water. Using cement for mortars and renders means that when it rains the cement brings the moisture through itself to whatever is behind it. Usually, when it stops raining, most of this dries out again – but not all, and not in damp conditions, or where moisture is present most of the time.

When problems due to the use of cement first started to show, the industry assumed it was caused by rising damp, and chemical injection of houses against damp was invented. In fact we now know that there is very little incidence of rising damp, and most damp problems are caused by other issues.[27]

Many modern buildings suffer from condensation problems – a direct result of using cement blocks, mortars and gypsum plasterboard, whose impermeability prevents the passage of vapour. Lime and clay actually regulate humidity and can hold excess moisture within themselves without becoming 'wet', and release it as humidity levels drop – they are hygroscopic. This also helps to keep indoor air quality healthy.

Lime used as mortar or render absorbs water when it rains, and as it becomes saturated this actually prevents moisture passing through it and so it protects the building behind it. When it stops raining, this moisture is released into the atmosphere.

Most are not designing for a 200 year life, as we do at Straw Works. We see houses built in the 1970s (out of cement) deemed unfit for habitation and being pulled down, whereas houses built by Victorians or earlier (cement started being used widely in construction after the First World War) are being renovated and continue to give good service ... until the effects of new gypsum plaster or cement pointing start to cause damp or condensation problems.

Restorative Demonstrators

The recently completed BREEAM Outstanding and PassivHaus accredited **University of East Anglia Enterprise Centre** is a natural bio-building with a focus on local vernacular and natural materials.[28] It has been designed to meet the environmental credentials of the client Adapt Low Carbon, a low-carbon consultancy organisation.

Local thatch and reeds have been used for wall cladding and roofing. The main structural timbers are 'Grown in Britain' from nearby Thetford Forest, whereas the main Glulam frame is Austrian, and secondary Glulam elements are from locally sourced larch. The project also includes repurposed African iroko desks and reclaimed English oak for cladding.

Recognised with a BREEAM Award in 2016, the building claims the title of the greenest in the UK, possibly in Europe and globally, demonstrating that PassivHaus standards can be achieved with natural materials. The Enterprise Centre is the 2016 winner in the built environment category of the Guardian Sustainable Business Awards.

The **Cuerdon Valley Park Visitor Centre** in Preston, Lancashire, is the first UK-registered Living Building Challenge project and the first to be designed and constructed following the Living Building Challenge imperatives.[29] The timber-framed, straw bale construction will contain no cement and be Red List material compliant. In addition to a public café and educational facilities, the Visitor Centre will provide office space for Trust staff. The project is a volunteer- and community-built project which incorporates on-project craft training in straw bale construction and other crafts.

Figure 5.8 Cuerdon Valley Park, Lancashire

WASTE

> Waste equals Food: A core principle of ecology and circular economy thinking.

The Language of Waste

Within construction, we have a language issue that needs urgently addressing when it comes to thinking and talking about waste. While we continue to use the word to describe potential resources, we will always be focused on better ways of dealing with 'waste', i.e. recycling, reusing and preventing it from going to landfill – and, to a lesser degree, avoiding it in the first place. Michael Braungart (co-author with William McDonough of the influential *Cradle to Cradle: Reinventing the Way We Make Things*) has referred to our tendency to use words such as '*reduce*', '*avoid*' and '*minimise*' as the waste language of '*guilt*'. But in nature there is no such thing as waste – only food and resources for the next cycle.

The domestic dump or tip has been rebranded the Household Recycling Centre to emphasise recycling rather than dumping, yet the construction means of recycling remains the '*waste skip*'. We have Site Waste Management Plans and Construction Waste targets with Waste key performance indicators. Language is important, and as Robert Macfarlane (who we met in 'connecting with nature' in Chapter 3) comments in relation to his book *Landmarks*,[30] '*Language deficit leads to attention deficit.*'[31]

The volume of resources we call waste generated by construction is huge; we target 6m³ for every £100,000 of construction spend. With a UK construction spend of £100 Billion this equates to 6 million m3 of waste. How different our attention to waste would be if we used the term '*resource skip*' or '*conservation skip*.'

It remains too easy for sites to remove waste for others to deal with. In the UK, despite the high profile WRAP campaign to reduce landfill by 50% by 2012, we failed as an industry to reduce waste to landfill over a five or six-year period.

Of the historical landfill sites, research from the British Geological Society suggests that 3,000 are at risk of flooding, climate change and coastal erosion, leaking pollution into watercourses.[32] Over half of these – many predating EU waste regulations – contain hazardous materials and asbestos, presenting a toxic timebomb.

Back in the Total Quality Management days, we were encouraged to seek out and address the root cause of waste, not the symptoms. We looked at the upstream processes and activities, through problem-solving tools such as Cause and Effect, Fishbone and Five Whys. These are of course still highly effective tools, especially the Toyota Five Whys,[33] which should be the starting point for any lean thinking or improvement analysis. The 1990 TQM studies clearly showed clearly that the root cause of much of the waste in construction was a failure of '*communications*' between organisations.

BIM will reduce waste through improved problem and clash detection, and improved communications and information sharing. BIM provides other powerful opportunities for waste elimination through Material Passports; bringing circular economy thinking to construction; incorporating previously used materials within specifications; and modelling lean construction methodologies and procurement schedules more closely aligned to factory or assembly line cutting schedules.

Site Waste Management Plans to Material Conservation Plans

Introduced through legislation but later rescinded, the Site Waste Management Plan (SWMP), a mandated approach to managing waste in construction, might well have slowed down effective waste management by focusing on improved ways of managing waste rather than seeking to eliminate waste. Targets that focused on reducing waste to landfill largely ignore the volume of waste being generated. In addition, SWMPs received only lip service on many projects in respect of forecasting waste. Many SWMP's do not use actual waste data from previous projects, hence failing to reduce waste through continuous improvement.

The removal of the legislative need for SWMPs should however be seen as positive, as it provides an opportunity to move towards circular economy-based Material Conservation Management Plans. These take the view that every '*waste*' item remains part of the construction '*food chain*', where every item once considered waste is viewed as a valuable resource for future use.

For new build and refurbishment works we need to consider the future use of materials at the early stages of the project. Encouragingly, we are now seeing expressions such as '*pre-cycling*' – the concept of identifying the reuse or recycling potential of materials at the design or project planning stages.

Material Conservation Management Plans

The Living Building Challenge requires every project team to create a circular economy-based Material Conservation Management Plan (MCMP) that details how materials are optimised throughout a project's lifespan.

The LBC's aim for MCMPs is to encourage project teams to have a collaborative and thorough conversation to encourage conservation of materials. It is recommended that the MCMP is developed at concept stage to cover the life of the project, then enhanced at the commencement of each phase as more detailed knowledge becomes available and specialists engaged.

STRATEGY FOR MATERIAL CONSERVATION MANAGEMENT PLANS: Inspired by and further developed from the Living Building Challenge Net-Positive Waste Imperative within the Materials Handbook.[34]	
Development phase	Agree material conservation approaches, strategies, roles and responsibilities
Design phase	Consideration of *appropriate* durability in product specification Design for Deconstruction plan (project strategy for each of the ten principles) Pre-cycling opportunities (designed future use of building, components or materials)
Construction phase	Construction methodologies and quality control Practical material conservation measures, and project logistics (handling, storage) Procurement strategies including incorporation of re-manufactured or waste-content products Material conservation performance targets (forecasting)
Operation phase	Potential for upgrading and replacement of components Strategies for repurposing or recycling components, materials and consumables. Material conservation performance targets (forecasting)
End-of-life phase	Strategies for adaptable reuse and deconstruction Percentages of a project to be recyclable or reusable Residual value of materials and components

Restorative Demonstrators

The **Waste House, Brighton,** was constructed on the Brighton University campus between 2012 and 2014. Designed to resemble a typical house, the building incorporates a wide range of common construction and household waste items, including toothbrushes, denim jeans, video cassettes and bicycle inner tubes.

The Waste House is designed to be low-energy and sustainable, providing a live laboratory for the university's design, architecture and engineering students. The building has won several awards and was shortlisted for the RIBA Stephen Lawrence Prize in September 2015.

Figure 5.9 The Waste House, Brighton

CARBON

'Carbon is not the problem. We are the problem.'

PAUL HAWKEN, BUILDWELL, 2016

Carbon's Invisible Problem

'*Carbon Couch*' Dave Hampton paints a picture of the impact of carbon.[35] He comments that if carbon was coloured purple and not transparent then we would be living within a purple haze. Or rather we wouldn't, as we would have taken action to reduce carbon many years ago.

Carbon's problem is that the impact and consequence of carbon in the atmosphere is not readily evident, and although just about every environment scientist now agrees the carbon increase is manmade, this fact is still being contested in some parts of the media.

Carbon is seen as the key performance indicator of built environment sustainability. Yet while the Construction 2025 strategy calls for a 50% reduction in carbon emissions by 2025,[36] we still do not have a good grasp on carbon management and reduction. Construction 2025 sees carbon reduction being achieved via a number of initiatives, chiefly BIM and Collaborative Working, through a *dramatically more efficient approach to delivering low carbon assets more quickly and at a lower cost, underpinned by strong, integrated supply chains and productive long-term relationships.*'

Embodied Carbon

Any detailed exploration of embodied carbons is outside the scope of this book, and many excellent books, papers and blogs already cover the topic. That said, the easiest way to reduce embedded carbon – as we see in emerging circular economy thinking – is to reuse and recycle buildings, components and materials. Yet we rarely do this.

With an energy efficiency model focused on reducing carbons during the operational phase of the building, means of reducing carbon through material extraction, recycling, transportation and construction are often overlooked.

The recent *Total Carbon Study* paper from the Integral Group, DPR Construction and others looked at the carbon profile through the life of a refurbishment project (DPR's Construction San Francisco Office) and reported a number of key findings.[37]

- For new buildings, it is critical to focus on reducing embodied emissions; for existing buildings we need to focus on reducing operating emissions.

- Looking at the total carbon footprint of a building, including reuse plus net-positive elements, could represent a significant change in building valuation and policy.

- Refurbishment led to a reduction of 70% in embedded material carbon compared to new construction.

- The largest reductions came from the use of high-mass and energy-intensive materials.

- The Time Value of Carbon is not recognised within the carbon debate, which '*signals the need for changes in climate action policy that prioritise deconstruction and reuse over demolition*'.

- Construction carbons are not understood.

Construction Carbon

As the Integral Group report and many others have noted, we don't fully understand the significant contribution the construction process makes to carbon emissions. Sustainability certification standards only require projects to monitor carbons arising from the construction process, not to take action to reduce emissions. Construction Carbon tracker, ConstructCO₂ indicates that carbon emissions from construction are 92.6kg/£1,000 spend; transport related to construction (e.g. delivering materials and people to the site, and removal of waste) can account for up to 70% of a construction project's carbon emissions.[38] With an annual construction spend in the UK of £100 Billion, that amounts to a huge 10 million tonnes of CO_2 per year.

Figure 5.10 Visualising volumes of carbon will help construction reduction plans[39]

In March 2015, carbon globally passed 400 parts per million (ppm) for the first time, sending shockwaves among environmentalists globally. A month later, a survey commissioned by Achilles found that, while 68% of UK construction firms stated they intended to address carbon emissions in 2015, only 40% had done so.[40] In addition, 74% did not monitor carbon emissions from their supply chain, where the majority of carbon emissions occur, through transportation and high carbon activity such as concrete production.

It was encouraging to see a recent UK Regional Framework Pre-Qualification Questionnare (PQQ) ask how bidders are meeting (or would achieve) the Construction 2025 Vision target of 50% reduction by 2050. This question must be asked in all bids, for all buildings, and of all organisations – and then, importantly, followed through and driven by clients, monitored and improved during design and construction phases.

Construction Carbon Hierarchy

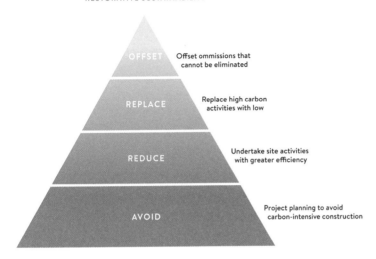

PROJECT CARBON HIERARCHY
RESTORATIVE SUSTAINABILITY

OFFSET — Offset ommissions that cannot be eliminated

REPLACE — Replace high carbon activities with low

REDUCE — Undertake site activities with greater efficiency

AVOID — Project planning to avoid carbon-intensive construction

Figure 5.11 Project carbon hierarchy

Every project should implement an effective construction carbon hierarchy, incorporating it into its core documentation (for example within the Employers Requirements, Project Execution Plan or Project Sustainability Plan). It is or should be regarded as one of the driving factors for construction methodologies and planning. And with travel and transport making a significant contribution, a project travel plan and hierarchy makes great sense for planning and awareness.

From 2 to 1.5

In December 2015, just under 200 countries signed up to the Paris Agreement, pledging to cap global warming at 2°C with an ambition to cap at 1.5°C. For the first time in climate change talks, the impact and influence of buildings and the built environment on climate change was fully recognised.

The Paris Agreement is recognised as signalling the end of the fossil fuel era, and the emergence of a low-carbon future. This presents a huge opportunity and challenge for construction, utilising all the tools and approaches we have at our disposal, for example:

- BIM to design and model low-carbon buildings and construction methods
- circular economy to reduce impact from construction resources
- lean construction to reduce all forms of waste
- education and advocacy to inform and inspire both the next generation and those in the industry.

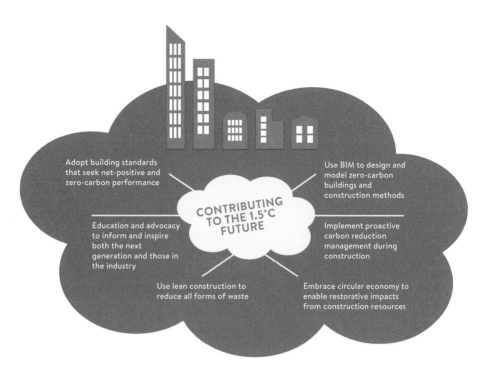

Figure 5.12 Contributing to the 1.5°C future

Offsetting

Carbon offsetting has received bad press over recent decades. I have previously labelled dubious offsetting schemes as useful as chocolate teapots.[41] However, in the wake of our limited success at reducing carbon, we now need to use all approaches available.

When (and only when) we have taken all measures possible to reduce carbon, we should then push for net-carbon positive, and offset through appropriate, related schemes. Evidence of carbon performance for a building must be holistic, taking into account the embedded construction and operations carbons, balanced out to demonstrate a net-positive result, with evidence of carbon offset.

We saw in earlier chapters the Living Building Challenge requirement for habitat exchange and carbon offsetting and the opportunities to offset through schemes such as UK Peatland reclamation.

Balancing construction, embedded and operation carbon

The 'Total Carbon Study' Paper[42] reports that in the US, 6 billion sq ft of new build is added to the building stock annually, for which the embodied carbon emissions would be 150 million tons, yet the equivalent operating carbons for that same area would only be 25 million tons per year. This would indicate that new build construction equates to 6 years operating carbons. And this is before the construction process carbons are included, something the report points out we have little real understanding of.

With new buildings increasingly achieving near or net zero energy in operation, over the next 20 years embodied carbons from new build could outweigh their operating carbons.[43] This indicates that in order to meet carbon reduction targets we need to shift focus in our carbon management, from operational to embodied and construction emissions.

Programmes such as the Living Building Challenge and the Living Product Challenge advocate for, and for certification require, the removal of fossil fuels from construction and material manufacturing processes. Reducing and removing dependence on fossil fuels in construction is set to be one of the next major challenges for the built environment sector.

Up to 70% of construction carbon is travel and transport related. Reducing such carbon emissions, through a reduction in construction fossil fuels is vital for both planet and human health. Carbon reduction improves air quality for construction people and for communities local to projects.

Figure 5.13 Taking carbon out of construction

GLOBAL ENERGY AND CARBON TARGETS FOR BUILDINGS

ENGLAND	Uncertain at present: The UK zero carbon new homes 2016 target rescinded by present government, but still subject to EU Nearly Zero Energy by 2019	UK Climate Change Act 2008 set a target of reducing carbon emissions by 80% compared to 1990 levels by 2050, with a reduction of at least 34% by 2020
WALES	Aligned to EU requirement. (All new buildings to be Nearly Zero Energy by 2019)	
NORTHERN IRELAND	Aligned to EU requirement. (All new buildings to be Nearly Zero Energy by 2019)	
SCOTLAND	Aligned to EU requirement. (All new buildings to be Nearly Zero Energy by 2019)	http://www.gov.scot/Resource/0043/00437438.pdf
IRELAND	Aligned to EU requirement. (All new buildings to be Nearly Zero Energy by 2019)	http://www.housing.gov.ie/housing/building-standards/building-standards
NORWAY	PassivHaus Standards by 2017	http://www.zeb.no/index.php/publications
DENMARK	Passive design and renewable energy use set for 2015 and 2020	http://www.epbd-ca.org/Medias/Pdf/8400SE16_2.1_11h15-11h30_Janssen.pdf
FINLAND	PassivHaus standards by 2015	http://www.epbd-ca.org/Medias/Pdf/8400SE16_2.1_11h15-11h30_Janssen.pdf

SWEDEN	Sweden's 'Integrated Climate and Energy Policy' (ICEP) aims to increase energy efficiency in buildings by 20% by 2020 and 50% by 2050.	http://www.gbpn.org/databases-tools/rp-detail-pages/sweden
FRANCE	New buildings to have net-positive energy balance by 2020	http://www.epbd-ca.org/Medias/Pdf/8400SE16_2.1_11h15-11h30_Janssen.pdf
GERMANY	Buildings should be operating without fossil fuel by 2020	http://www.epbd-ca.org/Medias/Pdf/8400SE16_2.1_11h15-11h30_Janssen.pdf
HUNGARY	Zero emissions by 2020	http://www.epbd-ca.org/Medias/Pdf/8400SE16_2.1_11h15-11h30_Janssen.pdf
USA	100% of all new federal buildings achieving zero-net-energy by 2030	https://en.wikipedia.org/wiki/Executive_Order_13514
CALIFORNIA	All new commercial buildings and half of the existing commercial building stock to be nZEB (Near Zero Energy Buildings) by 2030	http://www.arb.ca.gov/cc/ab32/ab32.htm
SEATTLE	All new buildings to be Net-zero energy by 2030	http://newbuildings.org/sites/default/files/OutcomeBasedPathways092414.pdf
AUSTIN	All homes to be zero energy capable by 2015	http://www.proudgreenhome.com/articles/austin-aims-for-net-zero-capable-homes-by-2015/
WASHINGTON	70% reduction in building energy use by 2030	http://classic.commerce.wa.gov/Documents/Commerce-Energy-Efficiency-Building-Strategy-Update-2014.pdf
VANCOUVER	All buildings constructed from 2020 onward to be carbon neutral in operations. Reduce energy use and GHG emissions in existing buildings by 20% over 2007 levels	http://vancouver.ca/green-vancouver/green-buildings.aspx
JAPAN	All new public buildings zero-energy by 2020, with a similar goal for private buildings by 2030	http://www.wsj.com/articles/japan-pushes-zero-energy-structures-1411745117
CHINA	40–45% reduction in carbon intensity by 2020	http://www.pnnl.gov/main/publications/external/technical_reports/PNNL-22761.pdf
SINGAPORE	80% of buildings in Singapore up to the Green Mark 2 certification standard by 2030	http://www.bca.gov.sg/GreenMark/others/3rd_Green_Building_Masterplan.pdf
SOUTH KOREA	Zero-energy buildings by 2025	http://www.scientific.net/AMR.689.35
AUSTRALIA	Net zero-emissions by 2050	http://www.gbca.org.au/news/gbca-media-releases/south-australia-on-the-path-towards-carbon-zero/36463.htm
NEW ZEALAND	Sustainable building tools	https://www.nzgbc.org.nz/
ARGENTINA	10% energy savings by 2016	https://library.e.abb.com/public/47c05cea99dc331dc1257864004ccc8e/Argentina.pdf
CHILE	Chile Sustainable Dwelling Standard 2014	http://www.worldgbc.org/files/7014/0982/5908/Santiago_-_City_Market_Brief_Final.pdf

PRODUCT	LIVING PRODUCT CHALLENGE	DECLARE	JUST	FOREST STEWARDSHIP COUNCIL
BRIEF DESCRIPTION	Re-imagines design and construction of products	Nutrition label for the building products	Social Justice Label	Forest Management and Chain of Custody certification
PHILOSOPHY	Regenerative	Regenerative	Regenerative	Reducing impact
CERTIFICATION LEVELS	Living Product Certification	Label	Label	Certification
PRODUCT, PLANT, MANUFACTURER	Envisions a moratorium on the insensitive placement of factories and on the extraction of raw material inputs that threaten sensitive eco-systems	A tool for transparently analysing the impact that a product has, in terms of Environment, Health and Manufacture and social factors	Just is a transparent tool for clearly analysing the impact that the manufacturer has, rather than just its products	Timber: Chain of custody Make-up of the product, and plant practices
ENVIRONMENTAL IMPACT	Restoring a healthy co-existence with nature through responsible place and habitat. Creating products that operate within the water balance of a given place and climate	Closely linked with the Living Product Challenge, the Declare label verifies if the product meets with the LPC Red List, a list of environmentally toxic and harmful materials	One of JUST's criteria is responsible investing (in people, community, environment and country), ensuring that the company provides a positive environmental impact	The main focus of FSC is to ensure that any wood harvested maintains the forest's biodiversity, productivity and ecological processes.
HEALTH IMPACT	Creating environments that optimise physical and psychological health and wellbeing	Declare allows the consumer to know if a product carries a health impact. It also imparts more information such as whether a component of the product is potentially hazardous under another classification such as an EPA Chemical of Concern	JUST monitors health impact both within the organisation and the community. It encourages products which contribute to the community, occupational safety to employees, and close management of hazardous materials	Prohibits the use of most hazardous chemicals and GMOs
SOCIAL IMPACT	Envisions consumer and industrial goods that allow equitable access and treatment of all	By announcing if the product is aligned with the Living Product Challenge Declare also gives the product a certification of how socially aware the product is	JUST's main focus is on the social impact of the manufacturer on their workforce and outside the company.	FSC also ensures that socially beneficial forest management helps local people and society achieve long-term benefits
INGREDIENT / RECIPE TRANSPARENCY	Endorsing products that are safe for all species through time	To show each component of a product, its manufacturer, life expectancy and end of life expectations	(Not focused on specific products but the entire organisation)	The Chain of Custody certification ensures that none of a product's constituents come from non FSC rated resources (does not detail exact recipe however)
QUALITY	The product must contain design features intended solely for human delight and the celebration of culture and spirit appropriate to its function. The product must be artfully designed and pleasing to use	Simply a guide for the components of a product, the Declare programme is not focused on the quality of the product	JUST's focus is on the manufacturer not on the quality of goods that they provide	FSC does not rate the quality of the wood farmed, only that it does not adversely affect the forest and its peoples
MANUFACTURER IMPACT	The product manufacturer must advocate for the creation and adoption if third party certified standards for sustainable resource extracting and fair labour practices within its industry	Focus on the products a manufacturer makes	Non-discrimination, gender diversity, ethnic diversity, committing to full-time employment, pay scale equity, being union friendly, providing a living wage, gender pay equity, being family friendly, and many other issues	Economical viable forest management ensures that forestry is sufficiently profitable without generating financial profit at the expense of the forest resource, the ecosystem or affected communities
LINK	http://living-future.org/lpc	http://declareproducts.com/	http://justorganizations.com/	http://www.fsc-uk.org/
AUTHOR'S FUTURERESTORATIVE 'RATING'	****	****	****	***

LIVING PRODUCT CHALLENGE
The Living Product Challenge is a certification for the entire life cycle of a product and its manufacturing process and impact. It aims 'to make the world work for 100% of humanity in the shortest possible time through spontaneous cooperation without ecological offence or the disadvantage of anyone' – Buckminster Fuller. It is a philosophy first, an advocacy second and a certification programme third. It achieves this through 20 different imperatives split into seven 'Petals': Place, Water, Health and Happiness, Materials, Equity and Beauty.

DECLARE
Under growing awareness of the health impacts of building product ingredients within the design and construction industry, material transparency and toxic chemical avoidance

are becoming increasingly important. Declare allows manufacturers to demonstrate their market leadership in transparency and toxic chemical avoidance. Declare also synergises with the Living Product Challenge aligning with the Materials and Health and Happiness petals and offers manufacturers an expanded point of entry into projects within the Living Building Challenge. Its database offers a transparent platform to allow projects to select materials to comply with the LBC.

JUST
Similar to Declare, JUST is a 'nutrition label' for organisations, allowing them to reveal information about their company in a transparent way. It is a voluntary disclosure programme through which an organisations works towards promoting diversity, equity, safety, worker benefit, local benefit and

stewardship. 'JUST is, quite simply, a call to social justice action'. The JUST goals are: to elevate the discussion around social justice in all organisations, to create a common language for social justice issues, to elevate the causes of those individuals who lead these issues, to change the policies and practices of thousands of organisations worldwide, and to make life better for people from all walks of life.

FSC
The Forest Stewardship Council is a non-profit organisation focused on the responsible management of the world's forests. It provides certification with two key areas: Forest Management and Chain of Custody. It enables products to label themselves with their 'tick tree' logo, allowing consumers to purchase wood products (such as paper) knowing that the production

PEFC	CRADLE TO CRADLE	BES6001	EPD	ISO14001
Forest Management and Chain of Custody certification	Cradle to Cradle Certified Product Standard	Responsible sourcing of construction products	Transparent declaration of the life-cycle environmental impact.	Criteria and certification for environmental management system
Reducing impact	Regenerative	Reducing impact	Transparency	Reducing impact
Certification	Basic, Bronze, Silver, Gold or Platinum	Certification: Good, Very Good and Excellence	Declaration	Certification
Timber Chain of Custody Certification for products and plant	Product, plant, manufacturer	Product / Plant	Product	Manufacturer
Ensures that the forest maintains or enhances biodiversity, and protects ecologically important forest area	Designing products made with materials that come from and can safely return to nature or industry	The traceable constituent materials (at least 60% of the total materials) shall be traceable to suppliers with a documented environmental management system ISO 14001	As a part of ISO 14025 Type III environmental declaration the primary / only concern of an EPD is environmental impact of the product	Ensuring that the company follows guidelines in environmental policies, the scope of the environment, the operation of the company, performance evaluation and improvement to the company the environmental impact is quantified and reduced
Prohibits the use of most hazardous chemicals and GMOs	Understand how chemical hazards combine with likely exposures to determine potential threats to human health and the environment certified	Operate in a responsible manner to protect employees, contractors and visitors		
Certifies that the forest management encourages local employment and recognises Indigenous People's Rights. Also requires companies to demonstrate compliance with the social requirements of the Chain of Custody certification	Design operations to honour all people and natural systems affected by the creation, use, disposal or reuse of a product	Requires documented management system for learning and development of its employees, and a commitment to consult with the local community stakeholders directly affected by the operations of the organisation. Continue to support sustainable communities by providing employment and economic activity through fair operating practices		
Similar to FSC through the use of Chain of Custody; monitors ingredients of a product ensuring that only PEFC-rated constituents are incorporated (does not detail exact recipe however)	Knowing the chemical ingredients of every material in a product, and optimising towards safer materials		It is just a declaration that the life-cycle environmental impact has been independently verified	
Again similar to FSC the quality of timber is not an area of focus for PEFC	The manufacturers' management system as defined by ISO 9001	Through association with ISO 9001		Through relationship with ISO 9001
Ensures the protection of workers' rights and welfare	Envisioning a future in which all manufacturing is powered by 100% clean renewable energy	The traceable constituent materials shall be traceable to suppliers with a documented health and safety policy and management system and follow OSHAS 18001. The organisation shall have in place a policy and documented code of business ethics		It impacts on the running of the business by monitoring the processes and then constantly and continually trying to improve them
http://www.pefc.co.uk/	http://www.c2ccertified.org/get-certified/product-certification	http://www.bsigroup.com/en-GB/bes-6001-responsible-sourcing-of-construction-products/	http://www.environdec.com/en/What-is-an-EPD/#.VkII567hDSA	
***	****	**	**	***

of the product has not contributed to destruction of any forest worldwide. FSC does not certify the forest management company, however it does serve to certify the organisation, which inspects the company.

PEFC
PEFC is the world's biggest forest certification system. Extremely similar to the FSC it serves to ensure that forests are managed in a way that allows all of us to enjoy the environmental, social and economic benefits that forests offer.

CRADLE TO CRADLE
The Cradle to Cradle Certified™ Product Standard guides designers and manufacturers through a continual improvement process that looks at a product through five quality categories — material health, material reutilisation, renewable energy and carbon management, water stewardship, and social fairness. A product receives an achievement level in each category – Basic, Bronze, Silver, Gold or Platinum – with the lowest achievement level representing the product's overall mark.

BES6001
The BRE standard BES6001 (also known as the Framework Standard for Responsible Sourcing) is a tool to enable certification against its requirements for constituent materials that have been responsibly sourced. It is relevant to any organisation that manufactures construction products. While mainly aimed at the business-to-business market it can also apply to retail organisations that sell construction products.

EPD
An EPD is not a standard by which to evaluate products; it is simply a transparent declaration of the life cycle environmental impact. It is an independently verified and registered document that details comparable information about the life cycle environmental impact of a product

ISO 14001
ISO 14001 sets out the criteria needed for an effective and usable environmental management system. It details the framework that a company or organisation can follow to set up a reliable environmental management system. It is available to any organisation regardless of activity or sector.

1   Edward Mazria, Architecture 2030, www.architecture2030.org
2   *Third Industrial Revolution, How Latteral Power is Transforming the Economy and the World*, www. thethirdindustrialrevolution.com
3   http://www.bullittcenter.org
4   http://www.bullittcenter.org
5   See http://www.archtoolbox.com/sustainability/energy-use-intensity.html for useful explanation of Energy Use Intensity
6   @lowcarbon-house
7   Terrapin Bright Green, *14 Patterns of Biophilic Design*, http://www.terrapinbrightgreen.com/report/14-patterns
8   Extract from CIRS Building Manual: http://cirs.ubc.ca/building/building-manual/reclaimed-water
9   Healthy Building Network: https://www.healthybuilding.net/content/why-materials
10   Gaia Group: http://www.gaiagroup.org/include/pdf/publications/The%20Domestic%20Chemical%20Cocktail.pdf
11   https://www.pharosproject.net
12   http://transparency.perkinswill.com/Home
13   http://ozone.unep.org/en/treaties-and-decisions/montreal-protocol-substances-deplete-ozone-layer
14   British Land Sustainability Brief for Developments: http://www.britishland.com/~/media/Files/B/British-Land-V4/downloads/investor-downloads/bl-sustainability-brief-2015.pdf
15   Ellen MacArthur Foundation: https://www.ellenmacarthurfoundation.org
16   Imperial College London: http://www.veolia.co.uk/about-us/about-us/circular-economy/circular-revolution
17   Douglas Mulhall, senior researcher at the Academic Chair 'Cradle to Cradle for Innovation and Quality' at Rotterdam School of Management
18   http://link.springer.com/referenceworkentry/10.1007/978-1-4419-0851-3_420
19   http://www.lifecyclebuilding.org/docs/DfDseattle.pdf
20   Declare https://living-future.org/declare
21   https://en.wikipedia.org/wiki/Asbestos#Discovery_of_toxicity
22   http://asbestosvictimadvice.com/2010/11/asbestos-ban-history-in-the-uk
23   http://www.asbestos.com/blog/2012/09/17/why-isnt-asbestos-banned-in-the-united-states
24   http://www.who.int/ipcs/assessment/public_health/asbestos/en
25   p17, https://www.gov.uk/government/uploads/system/uploads/attachment_data/file/422618/Digest_of_waste_England_-_finalv2.pdf
26   http://inside.sfuhs.org/dept/history/US_History_reader/Chapter14/MLKriverside.htm
27   The Society for the Protection of Ancient Buildings (SPAB) has some excellent research and information on this subject. See http://www.spab.org.uk/advice/technical-qas/technical-qa-20-rising-damp
28   http://theenterprisecentre.uea.ac.uk/the-building
29   http://cuerdenvalleypark.org.uk/visitor-centre-details
30   Macfarlane, R., *Landmarks*, London, Hamish Hamilton, 2015.
31   http://www.theguardian.com/books/2015/feb/27/robert-macfarlane-word-hoard-rewilding-landscape
32   http://www.independent.co.uk/environment/landfill-dumps-across-uk-at-risk-of-leaking-hazardous-chemicals-a6887956.html
33   Toyota Five Whys: see http://www.toyota-global.com/company/toyota_traditions/quality/mar_apr_2006.html
34   Living Building Challenge Materials Handbook (available from ILFI)
35   Dave Hampton: www.carboncoach.com. See also Slideshare presentation at http://www.slideshare.net/GreenUnplugged/dave-hampton-carbon-coach
36   Construction 2025: https://www.gov.uk/government/publications/construction-2025-strategy
37   Total Carbon Study: http://www.ecobuildnetwork.org/projects/total-carbon-study OR http://www.ecobuildnetwork.org/images/pdfs/The%20Total%20Carbon%20Study_FINAL%20White%20Paper_published%2020151113download.pdf
38   ConstructCO$_2$: http://www.constructco2.com
39   Carbon Visuals: http://www.carbonvisuals.com
40   Achilles operates Building Confidence, a pre-qualification and accreditation scheme; the survey included standardised questions on carbon: http://www.achilles.co.uk/en/about-achilles/news/2459-construction-companies-struggle-to-reduce-carbon-footprint-in-supply-chain
41   http://fairsnape.com/2007/06/19/the-inconvenient-truth-about-the-carbon-offset-industry
42   Total Carbon Study: http://www.ecobuildnetwork.org/projects/total-carbon-study
43   See Building Materials and the Time Value of Carbon, Larry Strain https://www2.buildinggreen/article/building-materials-and-time-line-value-carbon

CHAPTER SIX

THE NEW 'SUSTAINABILITY' STANDARDS

'"Compliance" is not a vision.'

RAY ANDERSON

THE PURPOSE OF SUSTAINABLE BUILDING STANDARDS

Sustainable building certification standards are immense influencers on not only the built environment sector but also commercial, industrial and domestic green lifestyles. With that influence comes a real responsibility in establishing the current direction of travel for the industry against a backdrop of climate, economic and social change.

Get it right and we move closer to addressing major climate change issues, attaining carbon reduction targets, and achieving ecologically, economically and socially just goals. Get it wrong and negative impact ripples far beyond the built environment sector.

While challenging traditional sustainability standards is now urgent and vital, it is important to remember that new regenerative standards start from different perspectives. The established certification standards (BREEAM, LEED, Green Star) emerged from an energy-environment-economics paradigm, whose key driver was, and remains, energy performance and prevention of damage to the environment, within economic boundaries.

New restorative standards such as the Living Building Challenge and WELL Building Standard are, foremost, philosophies, based on a set of ecological or health values. Secondly, they are advocacy tools, for promoting a better way of addressing the design, construction and operation of buildings. Thirdly, they are a building certification or recognition of achievement scheme.

However, it is the purpose of these certification schemes, not only to set 'best practice' for design, construction and operation, but to go beyond current best practice and establish a vision for 'sustainable buildings' based on what is required, with 'required practice' then measured against that vision.

When a Google search across numerous building sustainability standards is collated into a common set of aims and purpose, interesting drivers are revealed:

PURPOSE AND AIM OF BUILDING SUSTAINABILITY STANDARDS

To establish a consistent standard against which sustainable building design, construction and operation can be measured

To establish a best practice for environment protection coupled with economic and social development

To provide inspiration and aspiration to improve, reaching higher standard levels than the standard set

To enable the prediction, measurement and maintenance of buildings' sustainable performance

To give confidence to a building's investors, owner and users that an agreed level of sustainable quality has been achieved

To provide a standard to match building owners' and occupiers' green aspirations and values

To reduce CO_2 emissions and ecological impact and to safeguard human health and wellbeing through building design, construction and operation

Yet, if we apply the restorative sustainability that lies at the core of this book to these aims, we find the following:

- **Just being less bad is no longer enough:** A sustainability standard should aspire and inspire and then only reward and certify buildings that return more to the environment, nature and society than the construction and performance of the building take from the environment. Any performance gap between what is required and what is achieved must be positive: not just '*close*', and better than zero. Anything less puts the standards into the accommodationist's light green box of doing the minimum possible.

- **Best practice is no longer enough:** Sustainability standards should establish that which is required, not just incrementally improve good practice. They should challenge and inspire practitioners on the direction of travel required.

BEYOND EXISTING STANDARDS

The established sustainability certification standards may have served us well in advancing sustainability to where we are today. Or, they may have hampered progress, and not taken us far enough or fast enough. Either way, they need to be challenged by a new breed of standards based on restorative or regenerative sustainability.

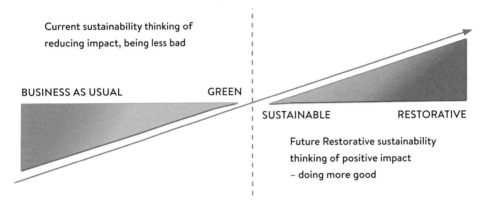

Current sustainability thinking of reducing impact, being less bad

BUSINESS AS USUAL   GREEN

SUSTAINABLE   RESTORATIVE

Future Restorative sustainability thinking of positive impact – doing more good

Figure 6.1 Moving standards into a net-positive zone [1]

This chart is important. It is key to understanding the philosophies of restorative and regenerative standards such as the Living Building Challenge and others. It represents the direction of travel for existing certification standards: moving beyond sustainability into a net-positive zone.

Within this powerful image, sustainability represents a Rubicon: once we have crossed it we can legitimately say we are 'sustainable' – giving back more than we take.

We need to flip the industry to *more good* thinking, through the influence of certification standards. From the climate change scientists' predictions, and in line with the 2015 Paris Agreement to cap carbon emissions and limit global temperature increases at 1.5°C, we do not have the luxury of time to do otherwise. Similarly, based on the predictions of climate change economists such as Lord Stern, the costs of addressing climate change will increase the longer we defer real action. We have to act now: we cannot afford not to do so.

Consequently, we need to stop regarding 'green build' as a benefit that we should be proud of. It should be seen as the norm; the way we build. Indeed, as a sector we should feel guilt about not using our skills and expertise to create green buildings for users and future generations. That we remain content to commission, design, build and operate buildings below this sustainability threshold reinforces the argument that the built environment sector is one of low aspiration.

The expression 'restorative sustainability' has been adopted throughout this book as representing the next, necessary step forward from the sustainability thinking currently prevalent in construction, enabling the emergence of a future level – that of 'regenerative sustainability'.

SUSTAINABLE, RESTORATIVE OR REGENERATIVE?[2]	
Sustainability	Limiting the damage we cause
Restorative sustainability	Restoring the capability of social and ecological systems to a healthy state
Regenerative sustainability	Regenerating the local relationship of social and ecological systems to continuously evolve

BACKCASTING FROM A FUTURE VISION

Reviewing the Living Building Challenge in her *Elemental* blog and in an article for *Building* in 2012, Mel Starrs highlighted '*backcasting*', which she defined as '*envisioning the end result wanted and then mapping out a path to getting there, rather than focusing on making current practices a little less harmful.*'[3]

Today, we find it increasingly difficult – intellectually, politically, economically and technically – to envision the future we really hope for. Faced with this difficulty, perhaps through too much choice, we lower our aspirations, content merely to incrementally decrease impact, rather than working towards a future where all benefit.

Built environment efforts need to become more responsible in addressing worsening trends relating to health issues, social inequity and environmental damage. The new standards give these elements equal or higher priority to energy and resource management.

A further fundamental difference is in the absoluteness of the Living Building Challenge. While there are different certifications available (as explored later in this chapter), it is a case of fully meeting the imperatives. In the case of energy performance, for example, this means demonstrating achievement design intent over a 12-month period. There is no scoring system, making the Living Building Challenge a clean, easily understood approach.

Built environment clients in the UK need to be aware of alternatives to the BREEAM family of accreditations – alternatives that may align more closely with their green, sustainability and corporate responsibility values. There is however a default expectation towards BREEAM, and an assumption that if we are not pro-BREEAM then we are somehow 'unsustainable'.

Working within the spirit of BREEAM, an increasingly common requirement from clients, is seen by the contracting sector as transferring the responsibility and cost of achieving the standard. This should be a good move, embedding sustainability into construction practice without 'just' chasing certification. Unfortunately, this has also given many contractors the opportunity to do nothing beyond the minimum required by Employer Requirements or through 'hollowed out' Contractors Proposals.

Existing standards may not as yet have moved the needle on the contracting side of the industry. Indeed, they may have actually hindered progress, relegating sustainability to tick-box accommodationist thinking, without conveying information about the wider climate change or carbon rationales for sustainability in the first instance (see 'Grey to Green' in Chapter 1). It is encouraging to note that services such as the Supply Chain Sustainability School, whose aim is to raise awareness of these issues throughout the industry, are now addressing the wider climate change and sustainability principles.[4]

REGENERATIVE FUTURES

'What if every building behaved like a flower?'

LIVING BUILDING CHALLENGE

The Living Building Challenge

Living Building Challenge 3.0 (LBC) is the International Living Future Institute's flagship programme for 'deep systemic change'. The Institute offers 'global solutions for lasting sustainability, partners with local communities to create grounded and relevant solutions, and reaches out to individuals to unleash their imagination and innovation'.

LBC's mission is 'To encourage the creation of Living Buildings, Landscapes and Communities in countries around the world while inspiring, educating and motivating a global audience about the need for fundamental and transformative change.'

The Living Building Challenge grew out of a mid 1990s project to develop the world's most advanced sustainability design project.[5] Further developed by Jason McLennan, the LBC became a codified standard (Version 1.0) in 2006. With Eden Brukman the standard was further widened in scope and developed as an international standard (Version 2.0) in 2007. In 2015 the current standard (3.0) was released after ongoing development and alignment with other ILFI programmes under Amanda Sturgeon as VP. As Executive Director of ILFI, Amanda Sturgeon was named by GB&D Magazine as one of the 10 most powerful Women in Sustainability[6] in 2014.

As a philosophy, an advocacy and assessment scheme, LBC has real significance. It enables us to cross that sustainability threshold, setting a vision for a future built environment and encouraging owners, designers, constructors, operators and users to track towards it. As noted regarding the opening of the Bullitt Center in Seattle, a Living Building Challenge project, such approaches are driving the wedge into the future by demonstrating to others what is possible. But it is a challenge in more ways than one: some of its imperatives would even be illegal in the UK, and it will certainly test current sustainability thinking not only in design and construction, but in funding, planning, and regulatory and legislative restrictions placed on the built environment.

> 'The Living Building Challenge is the toughest green standard out there, but it is seriously gaining traction as people get to understand it.'

LLOYD ALTER[7]

The Living Building Challenge covers four main 'Typologies' (Renovation, Infrastructure + Landscape, Building and Community) and, following the metaphor of a flower, is based on seven 'petals': Place, Water, Energy, Health & Happiness, Materials, Equity, Beauty, each with a number of imperatives. The ILFI web portal gives a comprehensive overview and background to the Challenge and should be a key reference for those in the built environment sector, sustainability practitioners and scholars.[8]

PETALS	IMPERATIVES
Place: Restoring a healthy interrelationship with nature. The intent of the place petal is to realign how people understand and relate to the natural environment that sustains us.	**Measurable outcomes:** 01. Limits to growth 02. Urban agriculture 03. Habitat exchange 04. Human powered living
Water: Creating developments that operate within the water balance of a given place and climate. The intent of the water petal is to realign how people use water and to redefine 'waste' in the built environment, so that water is respected as a precious resource.	05. Net-positive water
Energy: Relying only on current solar income. The intent of the energy petal is to signal a new age of design, wherein the built environment relies solely on renewable forms of energy and operates year round in a safe, pollution-free manner.	06. Net-positive energy

Health and happiness:
Creating environments that optimise physical and psychological health and well being. The intent of the health and happiness petal is to focus on the most important environmental conditions that must be present to create robust, healthy spaces.

07. Civilised environment
08. Healthy interior environment
09. Biophilic environment

Materials:
Endorsing products that are safe for all species through time. The intent of the materials petal is to help create a materials economy that is non-toxic, ecologically regenerative, transparent and socially equitable.

10. Red List
11. Embodied carbon footprint
12. Responsible industry
13. Living economy sourcing
14. Net-positive waste equity
15. Human scale and humane places

Equity:
Supporting a just, equitable world. The intent of the equity petal is to transform developments to foster a true, inclusive sense of community that is just and equitable.

16. Universal access to nature & place
17. Equitable investment
18. Just organisations

Beauty:
Celebrating design that uplifts the human spirit, the intent of the beauty petal is to recognise the need for beauty as a precursor to caring enough to preserve, conserve and serve the greater good.

19. Beauty + spirit
20. Inspiration + education

The Bullitt Center: Creating a Dialogue with Nature

'The Bullitt Center is about opening a wedge into the future. Once something exists, no one can say it's impossible.'

DENIS HAYES

Perhaps the best known of the LBC projects, the Bullitt Center in Seattle, designed for a building life of 250 years, achieved Living Building Certification in 2015. The building demonstrates an impressive array of net-positive and biophilic features, earning the project the title *'world's greenest commercial building'*. I had the pleasure of visiting the building early in 2015, and to investigate the stories behind the green publicity with Brad Kahn and Denis Hayes from the Bullitt Center Foundation. The Bullitt Center truly is an impressive sustainable building and has reinforced and informed much of the thinking within this book.

The Bullitt Center website provides much detail to the background of the project, including research into social value, costs and minutes from the design *'charrette'* meetings held as the design developed.[9] It is telling that the list of those involved in the concept stages reads as a US West Coast *Who's Who* of forward-thinking sustainability.[10]

Both Hayes and Kahn noted that the question they were most commonly asked by visitors to the building related to the cost of the project. The response, of course, depends on how you value the cost.

'Total project costs (hard costs, soft costs and land) for the 52,000 square-foot Bullitt Center were $32.5 million. As the first of its kind, the building cost more than conventional construction. With the benefit of hindsight, the project team is now confident that subsequent buildings – even those that seek equally ambitious performance goals – will cost significantly less.'[11]

In a Twitter-based interview as part of the Sustainable Leader Conversation series earlier in 2014,[12] I asked Denis Hayes why the Bullitt Foundation had chosen the Living Building Challenge rather than other standards. He explained: *'The LBC is [the] most ambitious metric for sustainability in built environment. It's hugely challenging. LBC Buildings sequester carbon, generate more energy than use, remove toxins from [the] ecosystem and promote human health. LBC Buildings have no toxics, compost all waste, use only rainwater and sun, they put water back into soil to recharge aquifers. All are natural ideas.'*

The WELL Building Standard

Wellness and health within the built environment has increasingly been an emerging trend alongside energy-focused green building. For many organisations, issues of wellbeing now demand as much attention as issues of energy and resource sustainability.

The WELL Building Standard was established by DELOS, as the first, and to date only, building standard to focus exclusively on the health and wellness of building and facility occupants. *'It marries best practices in design and construction with evidence-based medical and scientific research (the culmination of seven years of research, in partnership with leading scientists, doctors, architects and wellness thought leaders), harnessing the built environment as a vehicle to support human health and wellbeing.'* [13]

The fact that the standard grew partially out of health sector research and evidence rather than the building performance sector illustrates the growth in awareness of the relationship between health and buildings, given that we spend a highly significant and increasing amount of time within buildings.

The WELL Building Standard also has roots in Wall Street. In large organisations with high staff numbers, the staff-related costs have been found to be as high as 90% of all costs. It therefore becomes sensible to focus on the relationship of staff, and productivity, to the building's working environment.

Since energy can be as low as 10% of some organisations' total costs, it makes sense to remove the blinkered approach of treating building energy performance as the key sustainability driver, introducing instead a more appropriately balanced approach.

The WELL Building Standard comprises seven concepts, with stringent evidence-based requirements to address:

WELL BUILDING STANDARD	
Air	Aim: to achieve medically validated performance-based thresholds for healthy indoor air quality.
Water	Aim: to implement design, technology and treatment strategies in order to achieve optimal water quality for all internal water uses.
Nourishment	Aim: to implement strategies to encourage healthy eating habits for building inhabitants.

Light	Aim: to provide room illumination that minimises disruption to the body's circadian rhythm and provides appropriate illumination for all tasks.
Fitness	Aim: to provide building occupants with numerous opportunities for physical activity.
Comfort	Aim: to create an environment that enables occupants to experience comfort, both physical and mental.
Mind	Aim: to provide a built environment in which mental and emotional wellbeing is enriched.

The certification process includes submission of project evidence documentation and an on-site audit, requiring a pass level for each concept. A 'WELL Vital Signs Scorecard' accompanies the standard, demonstrating an environment's compliance with the WELL Building Standard.

PERSPECTIVE
THE EMERGENT CHIEF WELLNESS OFFICER
ANN MARIE AGUILAR & VICTORIA LOCKHART

There is a growing volume of research to demonstrate the value of strategies that deliver healthy buildings and businesses. With staff salaries and benefits typically accounting for 90% of business operating costs,[14] organisations are increasingly interested in doing what they can to foster more productive environments. With innovative technologies also transforming how people track their health and building performance, individuals are empowered with the data to demand healthier environments. The duty of care is falling to building owners, designers and operators to deliver.

The challenge now is to extend the breadth and ambition of wellbeing initiatives beyond people management and into the totality of the workplace environment and employee experience. For an authentic wellbeing message, organisations need to focus on optimal design and operations that aspire well beyond the legal minimums of safe, fit-for-purpose workspace. Our environments impact not only our physical health, but also our mental state and emotions: our spaces need to support tasks at hand, reinforce company brand and values, and facilitate healthier behaviours, ensuring that those behaviours best for us are also the easiest. Since it is the design, operation and organisational policies within a workplace that collectively shape individual experience, health and wellbeing, there is an emergent need for a Wellness Integrator to champion across traditional company silos, uniting HR, FM, IT and business in a holistic drive for wellbeing that pervades all aspects of the organisation.

The question quickly arises of how to measure 'wellbeing'. What can be tracked, and how can performance be benchmarked? Dovetailing neatly with existing green building rating tools, the WELL Building Standard is one early response from the International Well Building Institute. This translates seven years' research cross-cutting the medical and built-environment professions into a range of evidence-based design criteria, operational performance requirements and organisational procedures to support human health and wellbeing. One early pilot project – the CBRE Headquarters in Los Angeles – found 83% of staff feeling more productive in their new WELL-certified space, with 92% reporting a positive effect on their health and wellbeing.[15]

While the benefits of greater productivity, lower absenteeism, reduced healthcare cost and improved employee satisfaction and engagement are generally acknowledged as benefits of healthy buildings,[16] there is no fixed equation for the precise degree or a guaranteed ROI (Return on Investment) of each measure. The World Green Building Council suggests that outcomes are best measured through integrated data sets from FM, HR and finance: by combining financial, perceptual and physical metrics, organisations can identify key priorities for intervention and build their own specific business cases to track and monitor value delivered.[17]

This is also an opportunity to reinforce corporate branding. LYFE Kitchens, an American chain with a mission to 'Eat Good, Feel Good and Do Good', have matched their nutritious menu with healthy interiors.[18] UK developer British Land is demonstrating industry leadership by seeking to integrate best practice for health and wellbeing through their design briefs and operational practices, aiming to truly deliver 'places people prefer'.

As the role of built environment professionals expands to include designing the full occupant experience, we will see more and more new, interdisciplinary teams mobilising to successfully address both physical and non-physical aspects. Corporate organisations will increasingly discover the need for an internal point of contact for wellbeing. Echoing the development of the interdisciplinary Sustainability Executive position over the past 20 years, this Wellness Integrator, or Chief Wellbeing Officer, will develop and champion integrated health and wellness approaches to ensure buildings, employees and businesses are and remain healthy and well.

PassivHaus Standard

There should be little conflict or clash between the Living Building Challenge and the PassivHaus Standard. Indeed, PassivHaus should be seen as a viable route to achieving, for example, the LBC energy petal and net-zero energy requirements.

PERSPECTIVE
BUILDING ENERGY EFFICIENCY ISN'T ENOUGH ON ITS OWN
ELROND BURRELL,
ARCHITECT, ASSOCIATE, ARCHTYPE UK

The international PassivHaus Standard is best known as the world's leading energy efficiency standard for buildings. What is less well known about the standard is that it is also a comfort and quality assurance standard.

Energy efficiency can be seen as austerity: using less and suffering for a perceived greater good. PassivHaus takes a different approach and instead provides optimal human comfort for the least practical amount of energy.[19] 'Comfort' encompasses a number of different aspects that create an indoor environment people can thrive in.

Thermal conditions are a large part of the comfort provided by PassivHaus. An air temperature around 20°C can be economically and practically maintained at all times in a PassivHaus building.[20] And air temperature is not the whole picture; surface temperatures, including glazing, are also maintained within 3°C of the air temperature. When we are next to cold surfaces our body radiates our heat away and we feel cold, even if the air is warm. Cold surfaces can also create unpleasant draughts.

In addition to providing a comfortable environment, these thermal conditions eliminate condensation, which can lead to mould growth and associated health risks. The UK and New Zealand are among the developed countries with high rates of childhood asthma, which is related to damp and mouldy homes.[21] PassivHaus protects the health of the inhabitants.

PassivHaus also provides comfort in the form of a quiet, draught-free indoor environment constantly supplied with fresh, filtered air. External noise pollution is significantly reduced and the internal building systems are exceptionally quiet. The ventilation system in PassivHaus buildings provides fresh air from the outside, filtered and pre-warmed using the heat from the stale air being expelled. No stale indoor air is re-circulated.

Exemplary comfort requirements are paired with radical energy efficiency. PassivHaus buildings use between 75% and 90% less energy than a typical building. This is achieved through a rigorous fabric-first approach, including super insulation, high performance glazing and airtight, thermal-bridge-free construction, along with super-efficient heat recovery ventilation.

Quality assurance is the final aspect that makes the PassivHaus Standard a comprehensive and reliable method of delivering exceptional comfort and radical energy efficiency.

With buildings that need 75% less energy than most current buildings – this is also achievable with PassivHaus retrofits – we are a big step closer to breaking our dependence on fossil fuels.

The PassivHaus Standard sets the benchmark for what we should expect from a comfortable, energy-efficient, quality building. This is the baseline for all buildings that we need for a truly sustainable future.

AECB Carbon Lite Programme

The AECB is a step by step guide focusing on low carbon and low energy use in buildings built around PassivHaus standards in construction and in use.[22] The programme was devised and is managed by the Association for Environment Conscious Building (AECB) with an independent Advisory Board representing 'a broad spectrum of mainstream construction'. Aligned to PassivHaus standards in Germany, Switzerland and elsewhere, the programme provides three steps: Silver, PassivHaus and Gold. It pushes requirements from adopting widely available technologies at Silver level, via full compliance with PassivHaus standards, to best international practice at Gold level.

One Planet Living

One Planet Living is a restorative ecological programme devolved by Bioregional. The built environment, construction and regeneration feature high in the work of One Planet Living, to 'exploit' opportunities for making towns and cities more sustainable. As explained in their mission statement:

'The concept of One Planet Living builds on sustainability work carried out over the past few decades but specifically grew out of Bioregional's work to build the BedZED eco-village in south London. Living and working at BedZED and analysing its impacts drew us clearly to the conclusion that to achieve sustainability, we need to make it easy, attractive and affordable for people everywhere to lead whole sustainable lifestyles – not just green buildings, but wider infrastructure and products and services as well – all wrapped up in a simple and clear story which people can understand.'[23]

Based on ten guiding principles as a sustainability framework, One Planet Living uses both ecological and carbon footprinting as headline indicators:

ONE PLANET LIVING: AIMS AND PRINCIPLES	
Health and happiness	Respecting and reviving local identity, wisdom and culture; encouraging the involvement of people in shaping their community and creating a new culture of sustainability
Equity and local economy	Creating bioregional economies that support equity and diverse local employment and international fair trade
Land use and wildlife	Protecting and restoring biodiversity and creating new natural habitats through good land use and integration into the built environment
Sustainable water	Using water efficiently in buildings, farming and manufacturing. Designing to avoid local issues such as flooding, drought and water-course pollution
Sustainable transport	Reducing the need to travel, and encouraging low- and zero-carbon modes of transport to reduce emissions

Zero carbon	Making buildings energy efficient and delivering all energy with renewable technologies
Local and sustainable food	Supporting sustainable and humane farming; promoting access to healthy, low impact, local, seasonal and organic diets and reducing food waste
Sustainable materials	Using sustainable and healthy products, such as those with low embodied energy, sourced locally, made from renewable or waste resources
Zero waste	Reducing waste, reusing where possible, and ultimately sending zero waste to landfill
Culture and community	Respecting and reviving local identity, wisdom and culture; encouraging the involvement of people in shaping their community and creating a new culture of sustainability

Natural Step Framework for Sustainability

The Natural Step was founded in the 1980s by Dr Karl-Henrik Robèrt, one of Sweden's leading cancer scientists, to facilitate a consensus between science and sustainability, based on the observations he had made regarding the treatment of health issues and the addressing of environmental impact. He noted: *'Business is the economic engine of the Western culture, and if that could be transformed to truly servce nature as well as ourselves, it could become essential to our rescue.'*[24]

Based on four sustainability principles that originated from the necessary *'system conditions'* for health and developed into *'system conditions'* necessary for sustainability in society, organisations or projects, the Natural Step uses *'a shared language'* to develop a collaborative plan for change.

NATURAL STEP FRAMEWORK FOR SUSTAINABILITY	
Sustainability Principle 1	We cannot dig stuff up from the Earth at a rate faster than it naturally returns and replenishes.
Sustainability Principle 2	We cannot make chemical stuff at a rate faster than it takes nature to break it down.
Sustainability Principle 3	We cannot cause destruction to the planet at a rate faster than it takes to regrow.
Sustainability Principle 4	We cannot do things that prevent others from fulfilling their basic needs.

The Natural Step also uses the concept of backcasting, in this case using the principles to start with the end in mind, understanding what is required to achieve the end game, and then moving step by step to attain that vision. Creating a sustainability vision is undertaken through the Natural Steps ABCD planning process (Awareness, Baseline assessment, Creative solutions and Devise plan).

Under the leadership of the late Ray Anderson, the Natural Step was instrumental in shaping the global carpet organisation, Interface Inc's sustainability vision and model, known as Mission Zero, to climb 'Mt Sustainability', where the summit represented the sustainability vision of Interface and its aim to eliminate all negative impacts by 2020.

The ski resort of Whistler, in Canada, was one of the early adopters of the Natural Step, using it to define sustainability and to shape its visions and programmes in line with its most important asset – the natural environment. The resulting programme, Whistler2020: Moving Toward a Sustainable Future – a comprehensive community-owned sustainability plan – was used at all levels of municipal development.

FUTURE STANDARDS: COLLABORATIVE AND DISRUPTIVE

Traditional sustainability standards, and to some degree the newer standards, are built upon the thinking shaped by the 1987 Brundtland definition for sustainable development – the principle of doing nothing today to compromise tomorrow's generation. However, the sustainability world has changed and, as we have seen in 2015, the UN Sustainability Development Goals set out a far more proactive and ambitious approach.

If we in the built environment sector are serious about sustainability, then we have to embrace these 17 goals, and that means revisiting and revising our thinking, so that our standards become a responsible driver and influencer for a future that is socially just, culturally rich and ecologically restorative.

Given the urgency in transforming our built environment to address climate change, and to acknowledge the influence and leverage the sector has on other aspects of business and society, there is a need for sharing success. This is explored in more detail in Chapter 7 – but in the age of social media, sustainability certifications must embrace a requirement to share sustainability innovations and achievements.

A Collaborative Future?

PERSPECTIVE
STANDARDS COMPETING FOR SUSTAINABILITY
CLAIRE BOWLES,
FORMER PROJECT MANAGER, GREEN VISION

Imagine if all of the green building standards complemented each other and worked together to accelerate an overall improvement in the standard of our building stock and the quality of life for its inhabitants.

With a proliferation in the number and type of green building certifications and accreditation standards, it is important to understand why a certain approach should or could be adopted.

There are varied reasons for pursuing a green building certification for a project. Certification provides verification of the environmental nature of the project, and can be used as a valuable educational and marketing tool for owners and design and construction teams through the process of creating a 'greener' building. Such certifications can also be a powerful incentivisation tool for clients, owners, designers and users to develop and promote highly sustainable construction practices.

Four key standards are One Planet Living, the Living Building Challenge, BREEAM and Passiv Haus. They are so different yet complementary that for them not to collaborate seems an opportunity lost. They each offer a different approach to accreditation and certification of green buildings and attract support from differing client groups.

At a 2015 Green Vision panel discussion held during the Leeds EcoFair, a panel comprising Sue Riddlestone (One Planet Living), Martin Brown (Living Building Challenge), Martin Townsend (BREEAM) and Chris Herring (Passiv Haus) and chaired by John Alker (UKGBC) debated competition and collaboration between current building standards. While competition between all four standards is healthy, providing customer choice, it is paramount that they are comparable and set so as to enable comparison and collaboration.

PassivHaus is a voluntary standard that sets the bar for high performance thermal energy efficiency and comfort in buildings. Yet if we wish to look beyond energy efficiency we have to look further afield. The One Planet Living approach with a ten principles framework is a simple way to plan, deliver, communicate and mainstream sustainable development. Many of us are familiar with BREEAM certification of buildings, which is a programme that uses a rating score and third-party verification to encourage innovative holistic design. Whereas the Living Building Challenge (LBC) is a building certification programme, advocacy tool and philosophy that aims to rapidly diminish the gap between current limits and the end-game positive solutions we seek, taking into account material toxicity and social equity.

Both One Planet Living and the Living Building Challenge aim to answer questions that are at the heart of green buildings, where, in addition to energy efficiency, attention is paid to the whole building, its inhabitants, its relationship with its surroundings and beyond the life cycle of the structure.

While 'the building' is important, let's not forget the community, lifestyle, social equality, human and diversity issues central to sustainability. Without these considerations, high performing 'sustainable' buildings will continue to be produced using materials with high toxicity ratings and through unacceptable and unjust practices across the world.

The future of sustainability standards will eventually follow other sector-disruptive developments in moving to an inter-operability, open-sourced approach. We are not far from the era of dovetailed standards, where clients and others will assemble a certification standard best suited to meet their values, requirements and sustainability aspirations, instead of being pressed into choosing between existing standards and having multiple costly and often conflicting standard applications.

We are already seeing collaborative thinking between LEED and the Living Building Challenge, in the US, where the LBC energy, water and material requirements are now recognised for certification points by LEED. In addition, the LEED v.4 Materials Requirement is now closely aligned to the Living Building Challenge Red List, Pharos and Healthy Product Declaration thinking.

In a recent blog post, John Elkington articulated what many may be wondering: can we 'Uber-ise' sustainability?[25] The answer is yes, and the day will soon be here, when fresh-thinking, digitally-enabled, lean start-up organisations, unfettered by the 'traditional' way we have always done things, will offer alternative sustainability certification and recognition services that are tailored to the ever more complex needs of organisations.

Portico – a Google construction portal for its own building projects, which focuses on healthy materials – is an example of a major, influential organisation developing its own project standards and certifications. 'Constructing buildings isn't our core business,' Google notes on its Portico support pages, 'but creating work environments that inspire and energize our people is a major goal. The result: healthy Google buildings for healthy Google people.'[26]

This will of course disrupt and challenge the audit and assessment rules and criteria of established standards, in much the same way Uber has with taxi services, and that PayPal, Amazon, Google and others have disrupted other industry sectors.

But it is a disruption that is necessary. And in many ways the scene is set, with the digitalisation of design, construction and operation through Building Information Management approaches, the increase in Smart, Internet of Things technologies in buildings, the popularity of the LEED Dynamic Plaque and other real time sustainability monitors. All of which have the potential, individually or more rapidly through converging, to disrupt sustainability standards.

---

[1]   See Bill Reed, 'Shifting our Mental Model': http://www.integrativedesign.net/images/ShiftingOurMentalModel.pdf

[2]   Adapted from the Integrative Design Collaborative blog: http://www.integrativedesign.net/trajectory.htm

[3]   http://www.building.co.uk/deepest-green-credentials/5039725.article. See also author's blog https://fairsnape.com/2012/07/18/mel-starrs-sustainability-champion-maven-and-friend

[4]   Supply Chain Sustainability School: https://www.supplychainschool.co.uk

[5]   Epicenter in Bozeman, Montana

[6]   www.living-future.org/topic/amanda-sturgeon

[7]   Lloyd Alter: TreeHugger (2013), http://www.treehugger.com/green-architecture/great-graphic-explanation-living-building-challenge.html

[8]   Living Building Challenge: http://living-future.org/lbc

[9]   http://www.bullittcenter.org

[10] Optimizing Urban Ecosystem Services: The Bullitt Center Case Study, (EcoTrust), http://www.ecotrust.org/media/bullitt_report_7_16_14_high_res.pdf

[11] Bullitt Center Financial Case Study: http://www.bullittcenter.org/2015/04/02/bullitt-center-financial-case-study

12 http://fairsnape.com/2014/08/05/restorative-sustainability-once-something-exists-no-one-can-say-its-impossible

13 http://delos.com/about/well-building-standard

14 World Green Building Council (2014), *Health, Wellbeing & Productivity in Offices*, http://www.ukgbc.org/content/health-wellbeing-and-productivity-offices

15 Brian Barth, 'Building WELL', GPD Magazine. Accessed Mar 2015: http://gbdmagazine.com/2015/building-well

16 McGraw Hill, 2014. *The Drive Toward Healthier buildings: The market drivers and impact of building design and construction on occupant health, wellbeing and productivity* http://www.worldgbc.org/infohub/drive-toward-healthier-buildings/

17 World Green Building Council [WGBC] (2014), *Health, Wellbeing & Productivity in Offices*, http://www.ukgbc.org/content/health-wellbeing-and-productivity-offices

18 LYFE have in fact publically committed to pursuing WELL Building Certification for all facilities in their five-year development pipeline

19 In accordance with ISO 7730, based on the work of the Danish scientist P.O. Fanger

20 The World Health Organization recommends a minimum indoor temperature of 18°C, and ideally 21°C if babies or elderly people live in the house

21 See for example: http://www.asthma.org.uk/asthma-facts-and-statistics

22 https://www.aecb.net/carbonlite/carbonlite-programme

23 http://www.bioregional.co.uk/oneplanetliving

24 Karl-Henrik, R. in Foreword to *The Natural Step for Business*, ISBN 10: 0-86571-384-7, page xiv.

25 'Uberisation' is increasingly used to describe disruption to traditional businesses or business practices. The term derives from the disrupting effect of the transport and taxi service Uber on the traditional taxi business, through use of social, digital and sharing economy applications. See John Elkington: 'Let's Uberise sustainability': https://www.greenbiz.com/article/lets-uberize-sustainability

26 https://support.google.com/healthymaterials/answer/6076896?hl=en&ref_topic=6079430

CHAPTER SEVEN
A DIGITALLY FUELLED RESTORATIVE FUTURE

'The amplification of our
lives by technology grants us
a power over natural world
that we can no longer afford
to use.' GEORGE MONBIOT

SUSTAINABILITY AND SOCIAL MEDIA

If there is one overarching theme that has resonated throughout my career
in the built environment sector it is that most – if not all – barriers, problems
and failures have a root cause in poor communication. As a project manager,
I saw communication failures manifested in progress problems; as a business
improvement director, lack of communication led to quality, environment and safety
issues, and a reluctant embracing of improvement initiatives; and in my work now as
a sustainability consultant, I see lack of awareness and knowledge remain the prime
barriers for adopting sustainability.

Today's construction and built environment sector faces exciting but immense cultural,
societal and technological changes. A rapid escalation in the need for improved
sustainability, better information management and advanced construction techniques
is testing and challenging established practices. While these challenges can seem huge,
we have at our disposal a new and powerful communications platform, a new tool that
will speed communication, increase learning and sharing: social media.

Alongside rapid advances in digital technologies, Building Information Management
(BIM), the Internet of Things, and the curation of and access to data, we will see
new iterations of communications which lead us into a whole new era for the built
environment – described variously as the next industrial revolution or Industry4.0 –
all of which will fuel a new sustainability.

As I commented in a *Guardian* article back in 2011, social media is not a new thing,
but a new way of doing old things like talking and communicating and having
conversations, using new technologies.[1] There is probably no better tool (and certainly
none more accessible) than social media platforms such as Twitter for keeping abreast
of sustainability thinking, development, papers, case studies and failures.

Indeed, as Tom Standage argues, today's social media is simply a digital version of mass or social communications that would be recognised by Cicero, the Romans and the Johnsonian Coffee Shop crowd.[2] Our current anxieties about sharing and mass communication are the same as those of previous generations.

Social media and digital advances present both the biggest challenge and the biggest opportunity to really push the sustainability agenda. Social media and sustainability are both paradigm shifts, requiring different ways of thinking, collaborating and communicating. We can also see a common set of drivers and values within sustainability and social media: the drivers of learning, sharing, communities, transparency, innovation, advocacy and collaborative thinking.

Those who utilise social media in business are already transforming sustainability communications. They are demonstrating the new business drivers and expectations of collaboration, sharing and transparency, and weaving social stories around sustainability practices and outcomes. Social media has become a key ingredient of sustainability communications and successes.

Business users of social media are those that Lucy Marcus would call stargazers.[3] They are aware of what is emerging and happening in real time in the world of sustainability as it pertains to their sectors, while remaining grounded in the business through traditional management approaches.

Hashtags have become a powerful tool, despite being underestimated by (or even unknown to) many in the construction industry. Hashtags are a means of ring-fencing or filtering social media 'noise'. They have enabled an explosion in the reach of conversations, events, presentations, news items, newspaper content and TV programmes. Historically, unearthing key messages on a new industry initiative would have entailed travelling to face-to-face events and sitting through presentations, usually for whole days at a time. Presentations were accompanied by a set of poorly printed acetate slides, and conversations with key stakeholders were limited, at best, to grabbing a two-minute chat with speakers.

Today, through hashtagged events, we can not only pick up remotely on key messages and slides shared from the event room, we can also participate and converse with speakers before, during and after the event.

The rise of social media has led to a communications shift in the way construction industry professionals share information and participate in conversations. In many ways, this new social dimension – based on engagement, relationships and trust – is at odds with the historical construction industry approaches of competitiveness and fear of sharing.

We are seeing the emergence of a new 'connected construction generation' sharing information in real time across organisations, sectors and countries, and forming digital communities of practice. Good examples are the influential #Be2Camp (an influential social media community of practice, founded by Martin Brown and Paul Wilkinson 2008 www.be2camp.com) and #UKBIMCrew cross-organisation communities sharing social media and BIM knowledge.

Indeed, without engagement with a sustainability social media community that is so vibrant, well informed, well connected and generous with sharing, I would find it harder to provide strategic sustainability advice and support within my professional role.

Groupings of conversations with a focus on sustainability, BIM and collaborative working are creating communities whose participants are both 'Generous and Expert'.[4] That is, they are generous in helping others long before – and after – help is needed, and expert in that they are competent in areas valued and acknowledged by others.

In addition to the hashtagged community of practice, we can see a rise in the popularity of influence rankings and listings, often with a gamification that includes scores for engagement across a number of social media platforms. While there may be concern over the influence-ranking formulae, there can be little doubt that such listings represent the communities active on social media around a particular theme.

PERSPECTIVE
'SHARERSHIP IS THE NEW LEADERSHIP'
MUNISH DATTA,
HEAD OF PROPERTY, PLAN A, MARKS & SPENCER

The phrase 'Sharership is the New Leadership' couldn't be more apt when I think about the role social channels have played in creating a sustainable business. At a time when collaboration and transparency are becoming necessary and demanded from business, social channels provide ideal platforms to demonstrate both.

At Marks & Spencer, we recognise the importance of openness to achieve our aims under our Plan A sustainability programme. Be it via our corporate[5] or individual[6] Twitter feeds, our Plan A website[7] or the many blogs authored by colleagues across the business,[8] looking behind the scenes at how we are trying to 'do good' is something Plan A is known for.

We recognise that many of the answers to what we want to do under Plan A don't lie within M&S; seeking external advice and partnership will help us move from incremental to monumental change. This is why we have harnessed the power of social channels to crowd source solutions to our biggest challenges – we are inviting anyone to help us overcome these.

The days of business being cocooned in its own narrow world are over. Using social channels to connect with our customers, with each other, and with our existing and new partners is fast becoming a way of working for M&S to become a more socially, environmentally and ethically restorative business.

PERSPECTIVE
THOUGHT LEADERSHIP, SUSTAINABILITY & SOCIAL MEDIA
ANDREA LEARNED,
THOUGHT LEADERSHIP STRATEGIST

Social media – especially Twitter – continues to be underutilised as a thought leadership tool for sustainability. While early adopters and brands have clearly seen the beauty of using social media to communicate with consumers, I continue to be frustrated that more of the sustainable business community's deep and innovative thinkers are *not* diving in on the business-to-business perspective.

What keeps them from doing so may stem from a few misconceptions.

One may be that anything deemed social media gets diverted to '*communications*' or '*marketing*' teams, when at the leadership level it should be thought of as executive development. Another misconception may be that people are still not seeing personal branding as helpful to the corporate brand – which boggles my mind. How can the wisdom of your organisation's leaders *not* be considered a powerful brand reflection? Thirdly, the feeling of not having enough time to be on social media may continue to be a general hindrance. Social media participation, like anything else in a thriving business or organisation, should be seen as a professional communications practice to be prioritised in the 21st century. (This, of course, necessitates self-awareness enough to acknowledge that there are likely plenty of other things on your daily responsibility list that no longer serve a purpose.)

The idea of putting time into '*developing thought leadership*' is easy to leave to others.[9] Instead, looking at the process or practice as '*developing social engagement with influencers*' may be the better, more compelling, approach. My theory is that becoming known as a curator of great links among your industry's biggest thinkers can be a lot more fun and personally rewarding than working hard in other ways to be a thought leader. You begin to be perceived as a leading thinker because you actively and enthusiastically contribute to your industry's social media conversations.

I see influencer engagement as increasingly critical to sustainability leadership development.[10] Anecdotal evidence lies in my observation of a core group of sustainability leaders I've known and monitored for a few years now. Perhaps counterintuitively, the most successful Tweeters have seemed to emerge from within the constraints of traditional industries. Especially where few have yet noticed its potential, there still lies incredible '*first mover*' advantage in proactive social media use.

We'll need to hear more from that community as the world comes to realise how much expertise and knowledge in sustainability and the built environment matters. The most referred-to leaders in that field will be those who have long since developed themselves and their networks through clear and consistent participation in, and authentic contribution to, social media conversations.

PERSPECTIVE
SOCIAL MEDIA INFLUENCE RANKINGS
JIM McCLELLAND,[11]
PUBLISHER AND EDITOR

Contrary perhaps to first impressions, it is not primarily personal recognition or brand reputation that drives engagement around the social media influence rankings (although the competitive edge to scoring does boost interaction).

The big draw is actually a community aspect: identifying connections and peers within particular '*community of practice*' fields helps provide a platform for digital networking. In fact, many Leaderboard Players effectively use the Top 500s as contact databases and research resources.

Where gamification does however bring a benefit is by sorting the data into intelligence, through rating and weighting influence (albeit crudely). The Leaderboard format refines the signal-to-noise ratio, rather than simply listing a jumble of names at random. That is where the ranking adds real value."[12]

'There go my people, I must understand where they are going so that I may lead them.'

ATTRIBUTED TO ALEXANDRE AUGUSTE LEHRU-ROLLIN

Uncertainty regarding use is a key barrier to the uptake of social media within construction and built environment organisations. Given that social media is a powerful communication, learning, sharing and improvement platform, it deserves the same organisational focus as any other improvement initiative, with policy, strategy and leadership role model direction. Inadequate strategies, or lack of guidance, only results in a messy, cumbersome, ineffective and sometimes even damaging use of social media.

The fear of sharing too much – and specifically of giving away secrets to the competition – is often cited as a reason for not using social media. The same arguments have been used against benchmarking, collaborative working and other best practice improvement initiatives. In the 140 character limit of a single tweet, David Scott summed up two key reasons not to fear sharing: 'Don't worry about sharing your best info online, 1) Your competition knows what you are doing 2) People like leaders not followers.'[13]

This is a problem because social media is increasingly today's shop window. It is as much the means of communicating an organisation's sustainability credentials as the website was in the 1990s, and hard copy brochures and marketing departments were before that. Social media is now, for many, the first encounter with an organisation. It has emerged as a great platform for communication, advocacy, learning and sharing sustainability information. Communicating sustainability approaches and stories must – and surely will – become a key requirement in construction and building sustainable accreditations, as has been witnessed with the Considerate Constructors Scheme. Worthy of note is the Living Building Challenge: its Education imperative requires all projects to share their experiences, approaches, stories and results through project websites. This should go much further though, by embracing the power of social media as a real-time project advocacy tool.

Social media has rekindled the case study, and in particular the sustainability case study. Blogs are emerging as the new case study, written not at the end of projects but in real time, with stories and opinion, sharing success and failures alike. Social media is also moving traditional case studies into multimedia, offering interactive storytelling productions that go far beyond traditional 'what we designed' or 'what we built' case studies.

Social media is just one aspect of the digital age, albeit arguably the most visible and widespread – and it is aspects of the social-digital age that will have profound effects on built environment sustainability. Consider, for example, the now omnipresent BIM, the emerging Internet of Things, the growth of big data (collection, access and usability) and the '*Uberisation*' of many once solid market sectors. And it is these technologies, and the iterations and applications that they spawn, that will disrupt existing built environment sustainability approaches.

SUSTAINABILITY COLLABORATION IN A DIGITAL AGE

As previously noted, collaborative working remains one of the key challenges we face in construction. Whether it be collaborating to add value to project requirements, or to innovate and develop on sustainability approaches, we have struggled to move beyond simply working together. And when times get tough and collaborations are tested, we revert to the historical silo and adversarial approaches very quickly, as illustrated in the publication *Constructing Excellence – Have We Wasted A Good Crisis* (see Chapter 1).[14]

Collaboration is key to advancing sustainability. For too long sustainability – like most, if not all, things in the built environment – has been approached in silos shrouded by a culture of not sharing for fear of giving away secrets. An adversarial stance is ingrained in the culture of the sector. However, over the last decade we have started to add another layer of collaboration, a digital layer.

For many, collaboration in the digital age involves embracing new technologies such as Building Information Management[15]. BIM may well turn out to be a panacea for documentation collaboration, yet it may not offer the real collaboration opportunities that will move our sector forward. If we struggle to collaborate face to face in a physical space, then doing so through computer screens, or in virtual spaces, can perhaps only weaken what we already have. John Lorimer describes collaborative working as resembling '*glue*': construction is easy, he argues, as is technology; the hard part is the soft skill of collaborative working, whether BIM is used or not.[16]

(Almost) One Hundred Years of Collaboration

BIM is only the latest initiative in nearly 100 years of our collaborative journey. It is the latest attempt to improve performance across the built environment, through improved collaboration, within the digital age. And, as we are seeing, uptake of BIM as a collaborative tool is a stepping stone to a whole new digital world of faster communications, allowing access to data and technologies that will both enable and test collaboration.

Alfred Bossom, an English architect who, on moving to the US, specialised in the efficient construction of skyscrapers. In his book *Building to the Skies*, Bossom argues that the best designs come from a '*group of minds in which the architect is just another link in the chain*', and suggests that by collaborating on the layout of buildings and factories we could save 30% in industry costs.[17]

Our (almost*) 100 year collaborative working, value adding journey

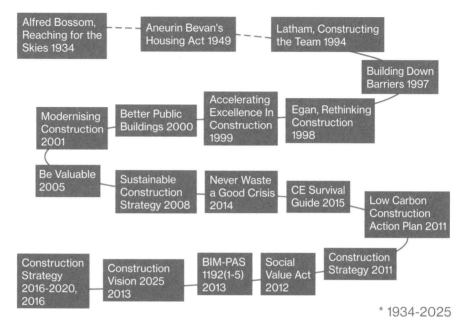

* 1934-2025

Figure 7.1 An (almost) 100-year collaborative working journey

We see this 30% figure appear far too often as the waste, the missed opportunity of the industry – yet it is really the cost of our non-sustainable construction approaches.

What is missing within this cost- and value-driven journey is strategic collaboration to improve sustainability. In 2012, Paul Morrell, who as Government Construction Advisor did much to pave the way for today's BIM and collaborative thinkers, commented that while Cash may be King, Carbon is Queen.[18] Through collaborative efforts to reduce carbon, we will also be reducing the waste – the Muda, that great Japanese term for all that doesn't make it to the final product or service – within the construction process.

PERSPECTIVE
COLLABORATION 2025
PAUL WILKINSON,
TECHNOLOGY CONSULTANT

In the yet to be published *Collaboration 2025*[19] document, co-authored with Martin Brown, for the Constructing Excellence Collaborative Working Champions, based on an open tweet-chat exploring collaboration, two scenarios were set up for 2025. In one scenario, collaboration had not moved beyond working together; in the other, collaboration had matured to mean co-development, beyond simply working together on projects.

The use and misuse of terms such as '*collaboration*' and '*sustainability*' featured strongly; optimistic views considered '*whole life costing*' and social cohesion, but pessimists feared continuation of adversarial, short-termist, lowest-cost approaches.

A vision for Collaboration 2025 sees data, constantly generated from built assets, as core to how we work. Data evidences our ethical procurement and our collaborative, lean and circular economy thinking, both in the physical and virtual spheres. We have learned to trust and to reuse data and information. Unconventional collaborations (e.g. with health authorities, charities, digital organisations) are now commonplace, and have pioneered new construction perspectives and innovations on healthy, regenerative, smart buildings and cities.

Restorative Transformation through Collaboration

The Living Building Challenge and related programmes promote advocacy through a spirit of transparency and collaboration. For example, in this spirit, red list compliant material schedules from projects are also available to other project teams. By publishing the materials lists online, new project teams will be able to benefit from and add to the work of earlier projects and, over time, accelerate construction product market transformation.

As we saw earlier in this book, every building is a potential resource for the next. Every building should be a knowledge resource, informing and inspiring future projects. Data now being curated illustrates only the tip of an *information iceberg* which can be made available in order to better inform restorative design, construction process and facilities management.

Building Information Management

Back in 2011, I wrote in the *Guardian*'s Sustainable Business pages that the biggest barrier to social media uptake lay at board and director levels.[20] It was also noted that the most dynamic step an organisation could take in preparing for BIM was to ensure that construction directors and boards understood the benefits of managed social media strategies, and would enable real open sharing and collaboration.

Green BIM

During a recent Green BIM conference, delegates were invited to present what they would propose to place into Room 101. I surprised the audience by selecting Green BIM itself for nomination. This was my reasoning:

- BIM (and related digital construction) is the most powerful of improvement and collaborative programmes for decades, if not in the history of construction. All BIM should be green; all BIM should be pushing the boundaries and doing more good, not happy just to maintain business-as-usual, a sustainability status quo, or be incrementally less bad.

- BIM strategy is a core enabler in achieving the Industries Construction Vision 2025 through sustainability and carbon targets – requiring net-positive approaches.

- The circular economy is one of the fastest emerging sectors within the world of sustainability, with a predicted market value of nearly £30 billion. BIM should be addressing the circular economy, in particular where one building becomes the 'food', the material farm, for the next building.

- Looking through BIM product data sheets we see products and chemicals that are scientifically proven carcinogenic – formaldehyde, PVCs, styrene. BIM should address these issues on health and wellbeing grounds.

- Green Vision, the Leeds Sustainability Institute advocacy programme, has embraced the Living Building Challenge, whose accredited projects (like the Bullitt Center) have no energy performance gaps. This is what BIM should achieve on every building, green or not – and fast. Let's seek a net-positive performance gap. This is Construction Vision 2025!

Lean BIM

> '... producing the right product at the right time in the right quantity for the customer and to produce exactly what you need and nothing more.'[21]

While BIM will be hugely influential in addressing the design and operation of buildings from energy and performance perspectives, it is when coupled with Lean Construction that real benefits are gained during the construction process, reducing and removing the Muda waste we saw in Chapter 1.

SIX COMPELLING REASONS FOR ADOPTING 'LEAN BIM'

BIM, in conjunction with lean construction, will get construction activity closer to that Honda advert expression 'Everything we do ... goes into everything we do,' ensuring better, net-resource-positive approaches. (Currently only 40–60% of what we do in construction goes into what we do.)

BIM, like lean construction thinking, forces us to focus on the endgame first – considering, for example, the project's sustainability, (net-positive) targets and sustainability values, and on pulling those through design and construction.

BIM, with Last Planner, can reduce firefighting and reduce the stress on project management team members.

BIM will drive lean and predictable programming and material sequencing.

BIM will streamline the supply value stream for materials, enabling just-in-time supply, improving resource efficiency.

BIM will greatly assist in improving information flow and communications between project partners and supply chain. Techniques such as the TQM/ Toyota '5 Whys' repeatedly show communication as the root cause of many, if not all, costly problems.

BIO – THE NEW DATA

One element to our mix of big data is a key dataset not yet on the BIM radar screen: data and intelligence gathered from nature. This is more than just learning from nature, but means understanding the inputs, outcomes and processes that nature adopts.

A further exciting development for BIM is its alignment with biomimicry and the circular economy, as reinforced in a recent *Wired* interview with Biomimcry 3.8 founder Janice Beynus[22] in which she shared her inspirational insights into near future manufacturing at the global carpet organisation, Interface Inc.[23] Asked what excites her about where technology is taking humankind, Beynus replied: *'I'm excited by the fact that we are probably the first generation to actually be able to gather biological intelligence and distribute it to the people because of the internet. Our understanding of how nature works is just increasing exponentially. Now we have a way to gather it and to actually make it available to people.'*

AskNature – the biomimicry experiment founded by Benyus – aims to get biological intelligence out to the design and business world, to share and aid understanding in how nature works, enabling us to begin to emulate it.[24]

PERSPECTIVE
THE NEW GENERATION OF PARAMETRIC SIMULATION TOOLS
EMANUELE NABONI,
ASSOCIATE PROFESSOR OF SUSTAINABLE DESIGN AT KADK

Regenerative and adaptive buildings challenge designers to embrace innovative thinking and multidisciplinary knowledge to deliver solutions that celebrate the richness of design while enhancing users' wellbeing and sustaining a living relationship with the environment around them.

Innovative sustainability concepts also challenge paradigms of modelling and simulation tools for design. Until now, software tools have focused on building energy performance and minimisation of environmental impacts. However, future modelling, simulation and analysis of restorative buildings involves multiple tools that connect domains such as ecosystems, climatology, material sciences, biology, human comfort and physiology.

Natural systems (such as vegetation and animals) can be codified and incorporated into design. Interestingly, parametric tools can be integrated with and mimic natural processes, so buildings could exchange resources from the natural environment (rainwater, wind, sunlight) while in turn enriching it.

Parametric tools in particular are being developed to integrate nature, visually and literally, into architecture and urban planning. The tool becomes part of the design methodology – enabling, for example, the design of buildings that can think, react and adapt to real-time weather conditions and extreme climatic events.

Whereas parametric design tools are predominantly used for intuitive sustainable design exploration, Building Information Modelling is utilised to support the delivery stages of a project by increasing efficiency and reducing waste. BIM has a strong focus on component-based delivery and coordination across disciplines, whereas parametric tools are more connected to the building design as a whole.

BIM is currently transforming the construction industry towards more component based architecture and life-cycle thinking. However BIM development, driven by business concerns, is slow and often lacks effective interoperability or the capacity for experimentation. It cannot offer designers a comprehensive solution for the design and delivery of sustainable projects.

Parametric modelling will significantly impact the way regenerative buildings are designed. While with BIM there is a risk that building performance will determine the character of architecture, parametric tools allow the designer to be innovative and at the centre of many disciplines.

The design sensibilities of architects, coupled with their unique ability to relate design to sustainable performance, social and cultural factors, will need to prevail over constraints of computing techniques.

A ZERO MARGINAL COST LANDSCAPE

We are, in economic and political advisor Jeremy Rifkin's thinking, on the verge of the next (and in his reckoning, the third) industrial revolution – one in which the dramatic emergence of innovations in the communications, energy and transportation arenas will converge to create a whole new human landscape.[25] But could this be our undoing? The previous industrial revolutions (steam, trains, printing in the first; the combustion engine, internet and fossil fuels in the second) have challenged our ecosystems to breaking point, showing them unable to keep up with our pace of change.

Perhaps one of the most dramatic outcomes of Rifkin's definition of the third industrial revolution will be the reduction in costs, towards a zero marginal cost economy. (Zero marginal cost describes a situation where an additional unit can be produced without any increase in the total cost of production.)

Construction 2025 already seeks to reduce building costs by 30%.[26] Yet perhaps a far greater reduction would be possible if we were to embrace concepts such as zero marginal costing, enabled by digital innovation and incorporated into BIM.

INDUSTRY 4.0

By connecting machines, work pieces and systems, businesses are creating intelligent networks that control each other autonomously along the entire value chain. The term '*Industry 4.0*' is emerging within discussions on BIM Level 3, and is a key component in the German government's high tech strategy.[27] Industry 4.0 thinking states that the first industrial revolution enabled mechanisation using water and steam power, and the second introduced mass production with the help of electric power. It was followed by the digital revolution that further automated production.

Whether we are heading into Rifkin's third industrial revolution or Industry 4.0, the warnings and opportunities remain the same. We can continue to be incrementally less bad using fewer of the same potentially harmful resources with more computerised high tech, or we can really harness digital power to do more good, aligning with nature through, for example, bio-data.

One route may lead us to a dystopian, *Blade Runner*-type environmental scenario that takes our already struggling ecosystems beyond the point of no return. The other may lead to a built environment in harmony with nature, one that enables us to start repairing our ecosystems and healing the future.

A FUTURE RESTORATIVE

As we see the increase of digital applications within the built environment, we will see a digitally fuelled restorative future.

This will enable collaboration, across the built environment and with less conventional organisations from the health and research sectors, that co-develops restorative sustainability approaches.

We have seen the emergence of the Well Building Standard based on real health data. The requirements and actions necessary to address health and bio- data will surely, in the near future, be included within existing building standards.

Digital developments will see an escalation of Circular Economy and Cradle-to-Cradle approaches based on data, with tracking materials across their life becoming easy, cheap and as common as emails.

A digitally fuelled restorative future will see programmes such as the Living Building Challenge embrace the reach of social and digital media to really influence the built environment, its clients, players and standards, such that restorative construction becomes the way we do business.

1   http://www.theguardian.com/sustainable-business/construction-sector-social-media
2   Standage, T., *Writing on the Wall – The First 2000 Years of Social Media*, Bloomsbury USA, 2013.
3   Lucy Marcus (2011): 'What it Means Today to be "Connected"': https://hbr.org/2011/10/what-it-means-today-to-be-conn
4   Bruce Kasanoff (2013), available at: http://kasanoff.com/free-guides/ which links to the document at https://dl.dropboxusercontent.com/u/47176869/Simplify%20Your%20Future.pdf
5   http://www.twitter.com/mandspress
6   http://www.twitter.com/munishdatta
7   https://corporate.marksandspencer.com/plan-a
8   https://corporate.marksandspencer.com/blog
9   See: http://learnedon.com/2015/08/influencer-engagement-not-you
10 http://learnedon.com/category/social-engagement/
11 Publisher and editor Jim McClelland manages a number of influencer lists on the Leaderboard platforms including Sustainability in the Built Environment, BIM and Circular Economy
12 See Chapter 8 for social media influencer lists
13 Tweet available at: http://www.davidmeermanscott.com
14 Available at http://constructingexcellence.org.uk/have-we-wasted-a-good-crisis
15 Building Information Management is used throughout this book as a generic term to include Information Modelling and Information Management
16 Brown, M., Akintoye, A., and J. Goulding, *Public Private Partnerships, Towards New Innovative Collaborations*,University of Central Lancashire, 2013.
17 Bossom, A., *Building to the Skies: The Romance of the Skyscraper*, 1934.
18 Referenced in Low Carbon Construction, Innovation & Growth Team Final Report available at http://www.bis.gov.uk
19 Constructing Excellence: http://constructingexcellence.org.uk/about/vision
20 http://www.theguardian.com/sustainable-business/construction-sector-social-media
21 A definition of TQM used by many, but credited to the '*father*' of the Toyota Production System, Taiichi Ohno. It is the basis for Lean Construction, and a key component of approaches such as Last Planner, Collaborative Planning and Integrated Project Delivery
22 http://www.wired.com/brandlab/2015/07/janine-benyus-inventing-eco-industrial-age
23 http://biomimicry.net/about/our-people/founders/
24 http://AskNature.org
25 http://thethirdindustrialrevolution.com
26 https://www.gov.uk/government/uploads/system/uploads/attachment_data/file/210099/bis-13-955-construction-2025-industrial-strategy.pdf
27 http://www.techradar.com/news/world-of-tech/future-tech/5-things-you-should-know-about-industry-4-0-1289534

CHAPTER EIGHT
FUTURESTORATIVE
RESOURCES

THE FUTURESTORATIVE ACTION PLAN

☑ **UNDERSTANDING THE CHALLENGE**
Identify five barriers within your organisation that are holding back your sustainability efforts. What is required to break down those barriers?

☑ **UNDERSTANDING YOUR SUSTAINABILITY CULTURE**
Where are you really on the grey to green spectrum? Where do you want to be, where do others see you? What is driving your 'sustainability'? What is your ecological 'handprint'?

☑ **RETHINKING**
Identify five areas of your business where your sustainability approaches could become net positive, doing more good, not just being less bad.

☑ **CONNECTING, HEALTH AND WELLBEING**
Hold a biophilia workshop exploring how your workplace, staff and projects could positively improve health and wellbeing.

☑ **NEW COLLABORATIONS**
Identify three unconventional collaborations that could really progress your sustainability approaches. Make contact and explore collaboration.

☑ **INSPIRE**
Identify five areas where you could advocate for sustainability in your educational and social media programmes – how will you inspire your staff, other projects, the next generation?

☑ **RESOURCE**
Identify five ways in which the resources that you use, or the products that you make, would benefit from circular economy thinking, becoming net positive and restorative.

THE FUTURESTORATIVE STUDY PROGRAMME

A module-based programme, based on **FUTURESTORATIVE** has been developed, for use online, in workshops, classrooms, lecture halls and forest glades. The programme takes students through a greater understanding of the concepts and thinking explored and developed throughout this book.

MODULE	AREA OF STUDY
	CULTURE AND CHALLENGES
1	Understanding of the tradition, history and culture along with the challenges that the built environment faces in making the transition to a restorative, sustainable sector.
	CONCEPTS
2	Exploring and understanding the key concepts for a restorative sustainability. Exploring the teachings and insights of thought leaders, books and publications.
	NEW THINKING
3A	Exploring and understanding the potential net-positive impact of the built environment on human and ecological health.
3B	Exploring and understanding the impact and influence of nature, earth, light and air on health and wellbeing.
3C	Exploring and understanding the impact and influence of energy, water, materials, waste and carbon.
	CERTIFICATIONS
4	Exploring and understanding the philosophies, ecological background and rise in interest and application of new, restorative sustainability standards.
	DIGITAL
5	Exploring and understanding the impact and influence of the digital age on restorative sustainability.

RESTORATIVE THOUGHT LEADERS

We all have heroes and gurus, and that's important. We are all undertaking sustainability approaches and adventures in an attempt to emulate or put into practice the thinking of those we respect. Some actions will be small, everyday and micro, others will be large, macro and industry changing.

ALDO LEOPOLD [1]
'Think Like a Mountain.'
Aldo Leopold (1887–1948), a US conservationist, forester, philosopher, educator, writer, ecologist and outdoor enthusiast, best known for Sand County Almanac. Leopold was a hugely significant influence in the development of environmental ethics, particularly between humans and land through his writings on land ethics, of seeing the natural world as a community to which we belong.

YVON CHOUINARD [2]
'Every time we do the right thing for the environment we make a profit.'
Mountaineer, environmentalist, writer and businessman, founder of Patagonia, considered by many as one of the foremost environmentally focused organisations globally. Patagonia's mission recognises the impact of business and aims to *build the best product, cause no unnecessary harm, use business to inspire and implement solutions to the environmental crisis.*

Chouinard founded 1% for the Planet, a member organisation of leading businesses financially committed to creating a healthy planet, by donating 1% of sales to enabling positive change.

JOHN MUIR [3]
'When we try to pick out anything by itself, we find it hitched to everything else in the universe.'
John Muir, a Scottish-American naturalist, author, environmental philosopher and early advocate of preservation of wilderness in the United States. His letters,

essays and books telling of his adventures in nature, especially in the Sierra Nevada of California, have been read by millions. Perhaps one of the most quoted environmentalist.

RACHAEL CARSON [4]
'The more clearly we can focus our attention on the wonders and realities of the universe about us, the less taste we shall have for destruction.'
American marine biologist and conservationist, whose book *Silent Spring*, along with her other writings are credited driving forward the global environmental movement from the 1960s.

RAY ANDERSON [5]
'Climbing Mt sustainability'
Writer, businessman and environmentalist, Anderson was founder and chairman of Interface Inc, one of the world's largest manufacturers of carpet. He is recognised as one of the leading business ecologists, whose zero impact legacy remains as a mission for Interface.

PAUL HAWKEN [6]
'The first rule of sustainability is to align with natural forces, or at least not try to defy them.'
Paul Hawken is an environmentalist, entrepreneur and author whose influential writings have shaped corporate sustainability.

GEORGE MONBIOT [7]
'The amplification of our lives by technology grants us a power over the natural world that we can no longer afford to use.'
British writer, environmentalist and political activist, a regular contributor to *The Guardian*, and author of a number of books, including *Feral: Searching for Enchantment on the Frontiers of Rewilding* (2013).

FUTURESTORATIVE BIBLIOGRAPHY

1 **Responsible Business** – Chouinard, Y. and V. Stanley, Patagonia Books, 2012.
ISBN 0980122783
Background to the responsible business values and approaches at Patagonia.

2 **Let my people go Surfing** – Chouinard, Y., Patagonia Books, Penguin Books, 2005.
ISBN 0143037838
Updated version expected Sept 2016.
Three books in one, biography, sustainability philosophy and business.

3 **Sand County Almanac** – Leopold, A., Oxford University Press, US, 1949.
ISBN 019500
Recognised as the classic for land ecology.

4 **Silent Spring** – Carson, R., Mariner Books, 1962.
ISBN 0618249060
The book that triggered the 1960s environmental protest movement.

5 **Cradle to Cradle** - Remaking the Way We Make Things – Braggart, M. and W. McDonough, North Point Press, 2002.
ISBN 0865475873
Groundbreaking circular economy thinking, challenging the way we make and dispose of things.

6 **The Tipping Point:** How Little Things Can Make a Big Difference – Gladwell, M., Back Bay Books, 2000. ISBN 031634662
Fascinating read on the business perspective of tipping points.

7 **Ecology of Commerce** – Hawken, P., Harper Business, 1993. ISBN 0887307043
Recognised by many as bringing ecology and environmental concerns into business.

8 **Wildwood** – A Journey through Trees – Deakin, R., Hamish Hamilton, 2007.
ISBN 0241141842
Living with trees, an autobiography from one of the UK's foremost environmentalist writers.

9 **Revolutionary Engineering** – Miller, M., Eco Tone, 2013. ISBN 0982690266
How the international engineering firm Intergral approach restorative sustainability. Included are case studies from their Living Building Challenge projects.

10 **Transformational Thought** – McLennan, J., Ecotone Publishing, 2012.
ISBN13 9780982690253
Essays to challenge design practices from the founder of the Living Building Challenge.

11 **Reinventing Fire** – Lovins, A., Chelsea Green Publishing Company, 2011. ISBN 1603583718
A route to a non fossil fuel future in four industries that includes the built environment.

12 **Biophilia** – Wilson, E.O., Harvard University Press, 2009. ISBN 0674074424
Part autobiographical and personal, Wilson's introduction to the love and relationship with nature that is known as biophilia.

13 **Biophilic Design:** The Theory, Science and Practice of Bringing Buildings to Life – Kellert, S.R., Heerwagen, J. and M. Mador, John Wiley & Sons, 2008. ISBN 0470163348
Nature-inspired architecture

14 **The Environmental Design Pocket Book,** 2nd **Edition** – Pelsmakers, S., RIBA Publishing, 2016.
ISBN 9781859465486
A go-to for environmental and sustainability design.

15 **Closing the Loop** – Benchmarks for Sustainable Buildings – RIBA Publishing, 2003.
ISBN 1859461182
How-to guide for measuring and benchmarking sustainability in construction.

16 **Eco-Minimalisation, 2nd Edition** – the antidote to eco-bling. – Liddell, H., RIBA Publishing, 2008.
ISBN 1859463002
Exposes eco bling and makes the case for ecologically sound and affordable sustainability solutions.

17 **Transition Handbook** – Hopkins, R., Green Books, 2008. ISBN 1900322188
The original handbook for the now-global Transition movement, addressing post peak-oil issues.

18 **Eden** – Smit, T., Eden Project Books, 2001.
ISBN 1905811276
Background to the development and principles of the Eden Project in Cornwall, UK.

19 Cowed - Hayes, D., W. W. Norton & Company, 2015. ISBN 0393239942
Fascinating insight into how cows have become a significant factor in human and ecological health.

20 Design with Climate: BioClimatic Architecture 2015 update – Olgyay, V., Princeton University Press, 1963. ISBN 0691079439
Reprint of a classic 1960s text that inspired and promoted architectural design based on biology and climate.

21 Biomimicry in Architecture, 2nd Edition – Palwyn, M., RIBA Publishing, 2016.
ISBN 1859463754
Insights into the world and future potentials of biomimicry within the built environment

22 The Rough Guide to Climate Change – Henson, R., Rough Guides, 2011.
ISBN 1848365799
A go-to reference for information on climate change

23 Biomimicry: Innovation Inspired by Nature – Benyus, J., William Morrow, 1998. Paperback ISBN 0060533226
Has become a, if not the, classic reference book for biomimicry.

24 Feral - Rewilding the Land, the Sea and Human Life. Monbiot, G., Allen Lane, 2013.
ISBN 0670067172
Inspiration for restorative and regenerative environmentalism and conservatism.

25 Third Industrial Revolution: How Lateral Power is Transforming the Economy and the World – Rifkin, J.
A future scenario where transport, energy and communication innovations converge for a new era.

26 Tools for Grass Roots Activists.
Gallagher, N. and L. Myers, Patagonia Books, 2016.
ISBN 9781938340444
Brilliant collection of essays and tools from over two decades of the Patagonia invite-only Tools Conferences

27 Landmarks – Macfarlane, R., Hamilton, 2015.
ISBN 0241967872
Why language and words are important to understanding our relationship with nature and landscapes.

28 Walden – Thoreau, H.D., Princeton University Press, 1852. ISBN 0691096120
Classic work on environmental and conservation philosophy.

29 What has Nature Done for Us? How Money Really Does Grow on Trees – Juniper, T., Profile Books (GB), 2013. ISBN 1846685605
How nature provides the vital infrastructure and services that keeps business going.

30 Last Child in the Woods: Saving our Children from Nature-Deficit Disorder – Louv, R., Algonquin Books, 2005. ISBN 1565125223
Why we need biophilia in our and our children's everyday lives.

31 Rough Guide to Sustainability, 4th Edition – Edwards, B., RIBA Publishing, 2014.
ISBN 9781859465073.
Useful reference text on all things sustainability within the built environment.

32 World Changing: a Users Guide for the 21st Century – Steffen, A., Abrams, New York
ISBN 9780810970854
A rough guide to global climate and equity issues. Described by American environmentalist and activist Bill McKibben as "the Whole Earth Catalogue retooled for the iPod generation"

33 Confessions of a Radical Industrialist: How My Company and I Transformed Our Purpose, Sparked Innovation, and Grew Profits – By Respecting the Earth – Anderson, R.C. and R. White, McClelland & Stewart, 2009.
ISBN 0771007531
The guide that shaped and continues to inspire the values and ethos of Interface Inc.

34 This Changes Everything: Capitalism vs. the Climate – Klein, N., Simon & Schuster, 2014.
ISBN 1451697384
How capitalism and our economic structures are at the root cause of climate change.

35 Cannibals with Forks: The Triple Bottom Line of 21st Century Business – Elkington, J., New Society Publishers, 1998. ISBN 0865713928
Introduces, among other concepts, the triple bottom line of society, environment and ecology.

36 Designing for Hope: Pathways to Regenerative Sustainability – Hess, D. and C. du Plessis, Routledge, 2014.
ISBN 1317626982
Explores regenerative solutions to built environment sustainable design through application of the Living Building Challenge.

37 Building Revolutions: Applying the Circular Economy to the Built Environment
Cheshire, D., RIBA. ISBN 9781859466452
Moving the built environment away from a make, use and dispose linear economy.

SUSTAINABILITY ROCKS PLAYLIST – TRACKS THAT INSPIRED SUSTAINABILITY THINKING

'If houses were trees … If buildings could smile …'

LUCINDA WILLIAMS

While the tracks in this playlist[8] may not have been written or intended as environmental pieces, the feel of the track – or even just a line – triggers the imagination and resonated with the author's thinking behind FutuREstorative.

> *If I Could be Anywhere* – Jackson Browne
> *Here Comes the Flood* – Peter Gabriel
> *Holy Ground* – Steve Winwood
> *No More Walks in the Wood* – The Eagles
> *What If* – Lucinda Williams
> *Urge for Going* – Joni Mitchell
> *Our Earth Was Once Green* – Runrig
> *Big Yellow Taxi* – Joni Mitchell
> *Where do the Children Play?* – Cat Stevens
> *Here Comes the Sun* – George Harrison
> *Spring / Birth* – Maddy Prior

Jackson Browne, a stalwart of protest, sings in *If I Could be Anywhere* of there being no better place to be than today to change the outcome of the planet, in a Gaia-influenced track that predicts the earth will rid itself of our greed.

Many of the tracks listed here protest against damage to the environment, from Joni Mitchell's seminal *Big Yellow Taxi*, to The Eagles' *No More Walk in the Woods*, inspired by Thoreau's Walden Woods. Cat Stevens back in the 1970s asked, as we sadly still do, '*Where do the children play*' as we '*build over grassland and countryside, as skyscrapers crack the skies*', foretelling of the Internet of Things perhaps with '*switch on summer from a slot machine*'.

Lucinda Williams' *What If* imagines buildings that smile, conjuring images of happy living buildings, yet '*windows that could cry*' conjures images of our unsustainable existing buildings and many of those we sadly still build today. Another Joni Mitchell track included here, *Urge for Going*, has a feel of connectivity with nature, having an urge for flying south when the grass turns brown. But it's not all doom and gloom. George Harrison's *Here Comes the Sun* and Maddy Prior's *Spring* paint a picture of hope, of rebirth and a new living future.

FUTURESTORATIVE CONTRIBUTORS

(Text, interviews, quotes, foreword)

Ann Marie Aguilar,
Arup Associates, @amsustchange
Associate Director, Wellbeing and Sustainability,
Arup Associates. @arupassociates. London, UK

Jenni Barrett, UCLAN, @Meme_Cloud
Senior Lecturer, Researcher and Consultant,
School of Architecture, UCLAN, focusing
on Interdisciplinary Design process, Social
Psychology and Collaboration. Lancashire, UK.

Carlo Battisti, Macro Design Studio, @battisti_c
Sustainable Innovation Manager. Project
Manager @TISbz. Co-owner @macrodesignit.
Founder and facilitator @LBCItaly. http:// www.
Macrodesign.it. Bolzano, Italy

Claire Bowles, @bowles_claire
Project Manager. Network Manager. Mindfulness
practitioner. Aspiring to bring about change for
the better in professional circles and family life.
Melbourne, AUS

Elrond Burrell,
Associate ArchtypeUK, @ElrondBurrell
Elrond Burrell is an architect and blogger
with over 18 years experience designing and
delivering exceptional sustainable architecture.
His specialisms are PassivHaus and Timber
architecture. http://elrondburrell.com.
Herefordshire, UK

Joe Clancy, @G_reen_I_Joe
Landscape architect, biophilic designer and
member of the LI's editorial advisory panel.
Founder of the @_NatureFactory. http://www.
designingthelandscape.com Birmingham, UK.

Sue Clark, Sweden GBC, @swedengbc
LEED Manager at Sweden Green Building Council.
http://www.sgbc.se. Stockholm, Sweden

Munish Datta, Marks & Spencer, @munishdatta
Head of Property and Facilities Management
Plan A at Marks and Spencer https://corporate.
marksandspencer.com/plan-a Senior Associate @
cisl_ cambridge. Cambridge, UK.

Chris Downe
Mechanical Engineering Graduate. Researcher.
Contributions to FutuREstorative tables
and matrices. http://linkedin.com/in/chris-
downe-781277104. Lancashire, UK

Soo Downe OBE, UCLAN
Professor in Midwifery Studies in the School of
Community Health and Midwifery at UCLAN,
interested in the utility of complexity theory
in understanding dynamic health states and
understanding the nature of positive wellbeing
(salutogenesis) as opposed to simply reducing
pathology. http://www.uclan.ac.uk. Lancashire, UK

Denis Hayes,
Bullitt Center Foundation, @denishayes
Solar energy evangelist. Environmental pioneer.
President of Bullitt.org. Developer of @
BullittCenter. Chair of @EarthDayNetwork.
Seattle, US

Barbara Jones, Straw Works, @strawworks
Leading UK company for design, building and
training with strawbale and natural materials.
http://www.strawworks.co.uk. Yorkshire, UK

Brad Kahn – Groundwork Strategies / Bullitt
Center @hbkahn
Principal and Communications consultant
at Groundwork Strategies. www.
groundworkstrategies.com.
Communications director at Forest Stewardship
Council (FSC) U.S. Seattle, USA.

Andrea Learned,
Thought Leadership Strategist, @andrealearned
Andrea Learned helps business and non profit
executives develop authentic thought leadership
and engage effectively across digital and social
media. http://learnedon.com. Seattle, US

Victoria Lockhart, Arup Associates, @vicki572
Wellbeing and sustainability specialist at Arup
Associates. Sustainability consultant for the built
environment. http://www.wellbydesign.co.uk.
London, UK

Jim McClelland,
McClelland Media Ltd, @SustMeme
Sustainable Futurist, Publisher, Editor, Journalist,
Speaker. www.sustmeme.com. Lancashire, UK

Christine Mondor, EvolveEA, @evolveEA
Christine is an eternal optimist regarding
the power of design in shaping a sustainable
environment. Christine has been active in shaping
places, processes and organisations nationally and
internationally for over 15 years through her work
as an architect, educator and activist. http://www.
evolveea.com/work/christine-mondor. Pittsburgh, US

Emanule Naboni, @EmanuleNaboni
Associate Professor of Sustainable Design at The
Royal Danish Academy of Fine Arts, Schools of
Architecture, Design and Conservation (KADK).
Founder of e3lab.org Copenhagen, Denmark.

Anne Parker, @itdoesnthavetohurt
Anne Parker is a self-employed coach, trainer,
project manager, consultant and mindfulness
practitioner. anneparker.co.uk. Lancashire, UK

Guy Parker, Conlon Construction, @_conlon_
Managing Director, Conlon Construction.
Lancashire, UK

Sofie Pelsmakers,
Environmental Architect, @SofiePelsmakers
Sofie is an Environmental Architect, lecturer
in environmental design at Sheffield School of
Architecture and doctoral researcher at the UCL
Energy Institute, co-founder of Architecture for
Change and author of *The Environmental Design
Pocketbook*. http://www.sofiepelsmakers.com.
London, UK

Amanda Sturgeon, ILFI @AmandaSturgeon
FAIA, Chief Executive Officer, International Living
Future Institute, @living_future @livingbuilding
Amanda has a strong passion for biomimicry that
influences her approach to sustainability. In 2014
she was named by GB&D Magazine as one of the
10 most powerful women in sustainability.
Seattle, USA

Claire Thirlwall,
Thirlwall Associates @thirlwallassoc
Claire Thirlwall is director of landscape
architecture practice at Thirlwall Associates,
specialising in river restoration and other water
management projects. http://www.thirlwall-
associates.co.uk. Oxfordshire, UK

Alison Watson,
Class Of Your Own, @classofyourown
MD of Class Of Your Own; creator of Design
Engineer Construct! (and other cool stuff!) to help
industry and education inspire future professionals.
BIM4Education supporter. http://www.
Designengineerconstruct.com. Lancashire, UK

Alex Whitcroft, @alexwhitcroft
Architect with a focus on environmentally and
socio-economically sustainable design. Associate
Director at Bere Architects, Architecture lead at
WikiHouse Foundation. London, UK

Paul Wilkinson, PWCom, @EEPaul
Consultant specialising in technology (particularly
construction software applications, SaaS, BIM,
mobile) and public relations, marketing and
social media in the architecture, engineering,
construction (AEC) and property sectors. pwcom.
co.uk. London, UK

RESTORATIVE DEMONSTRATORS

Table 8.1 Case Studies, Mentions and Inspirations

The following table gives examples of buildings, projects and activities that have provided inspiration. Many have been visited in connection with this book and are included as examples or case studies throughout FutuREstorative.

Project	Description (from Building website pages)	Sector	Theme	Building web link [9]	Building Twitter account
Bullitt Center, Seattle, WA, US	'The greenest commercial building in the world. The goal of the Bullitt Center is to drive change in the marketplace faster and further by showing what's possible today. The era of harm reduction, half steps and lesser evils is behind us. As a society, we need to be bold in ways that were once unimaginable.'	Commercial	Water, energy	http://www.bullittcenter.org	@Bullitt_Center
Cuerdon Valley Park, Preston, UK	The design concept is driven by the desire not only to minimise the impact of fossil fuel energy reserves during the building phase but also to consume minimal fossil fuel energy during the lifetime of the building. Local materials will be used where possible and those selected will have low embodied energy. UK first LBC registered project.	Public	Natural materials	http://cuerdenvalleypark.org.uk/visitor-centre-details	@CuerdenValleyPk
East Anglia University, UK	The original design for the University of East Anglia campus, by Denys Lasdun, allowed for a merging of the natural with the built environment. UEA now balances the 1960s concrete legacy buildings with newer, low-carbon additions. BREEAM Outstanding.	Education	Natural materials	http://theenterprisecentre.uea.ac.uk/the-building	@lowcarbonspace
CIRS, Vancouver, BC, Canada	The Centre for Interactive Research on Sustainability (CIRS) was developed in response to the challenge of creating a more sustainable built environment. Its intention is to be an internationally recognised research institution that accelerates the adoption of sustainable building technologies and sustainable urban development practices in society.	Education	Water, timber	http://cirs.ubc.ca	@SustainUBC
Squamish Adventure Centre, BC, Canada	'The Squamish Adventure Centre is a striking example of advanced wood technology and the capabilities of British Columbia's timber frame industry. It shows how modern designs with complex geometries can be quickly and economically built.'	Public	Timber	http://www.adventurecentre.ca http://www.naturallywood.com/sites/default/files/Squamish-Adventure-Centre-Case-Study.pdf	@SquamishAC

Squamish Environmental Learning Centre	Surrounded by towering cedar trees and flanked by the Cheakamus River, the BlueShore Financial Environmental Learning Centre (ELC) is a showcase for green building innovation.	Education	Timber	http://www.cheakamuscentre.ca	@CheakamusCentre
Van Dusen, Vancouver, Canada	An award-winning, 'Living Building' Visitor Centre. The building is widely recognised as a pioneering structure in green design – and is LEED Platinum certified.	Public	Materials	http://vandusengarden.org/about	@vandusengdn
Phipps Conservatory, Pittsburgh, US	A world leader in sustainable innovation, Phipps Conservatory and Botanical Gardens has achieved the Living Building Challenge for its Center for Sustainable Landscapes (CSL), a facility that houses ground-breaking sustainability research and science education programmes, and serves as a key part of the public garden's immersive visitor experience. LBC, LEED Platinum and WELL Building certifications.	Public		https://phipps.conservatory.org/green-innovation/at-phipps/center-for-sustainable-landscapes	@phippsgreen
LBC Project, Taneatua, New Zealand	Designed to the stringent criteria of the international Living Building Challenge (LBC), the completed project is New Zealand's most advanced sustainable building.	Community	Community, spirit	http://www.jasmax.com/work/te-uru-taumatua/ Video: https://www.youtube.com/watch?v=LwQV9fNQsDk	@tuhoeetu
Midge Hole, Design Comp, UCLAN, UK	A student design competition to design a residence for a live client on complex and isolated terrain while complying to Living Building Challenge rules.	Education, housing	Education	https://jennibarrett.files.wordpress.com/2014/05/josh-allington11.jpg	
The Crystal, London, UK	The Crystal in London is home to the world's largest exhibition on the future of cities, as well as one of the world's most sustainable buildings and events venues. BREEAM Outstanding.	Commercial	Energy	https://www.thecrystal.org	@thecrystalorg
The Edge, Amsterdam	The greenest, most intelligent building in the world. By employing innovative smart technology it has achieved a BREEAM Outstanding score of 98.36%.	Commercial	Energy	http://www2.deloitte.com/global/en/pages/about-deloitte/articles/gx-the-edge-of-tomorrow.html	
Zero Carbon House, Cardiff, UK	The UK's first purpose-built energy smart house, capable of exporting more energy than it uses.	Housing	Energy	http://www.cardiff.ac.uk/news/view/122063-smart-carbon-positive-energy-house	@zerohouse
Dyson Centre for Neonatal Care, RUH, Bath, UK	The £6.1 million Dyson Neonatal Care opened on 23 July 2011 and is an environmentally sustainable design, which is the first of its type in Europe. It is designed to provide a beneficial healing environment for babies and reduce stress levels experienced by their parents.	Health	Wellbeing, light	http://www.ruh.nhs.uk/patients/services/wards/neonatal_intensive_care/index.asp?menu_id=1	
Romarzollo School, Arco, Italy	The first LEED Platinum School outside the US.	Education	Energy	http://www.macrodesignstudio.it/en/services/projects	
LILAC, Leeds, UK	An affordable strawbale housing community in Bramley, LILAC is the UK's first affordable ecological co-housing project.	Housing	Co-housing	http://www.lilac.coop	@lilacleeds

Hanham Hall, Bristol, UK	One of the flagship Carbon Challenge schemes and will be England's first large-scale housing scheme to achieve the 2016 zero-carbon standard.	Housing	Eco village	http://www.barrattdevelopments.co.uk/showcase/hanham-hall-bristol	
Keynsham Civic Centre, UK	The building is on course to achieving an exemplary display energy certificate (DEC) 'A' rating in 2017 once it has been in use for two years, thus making it one of the lowest energy consuming public buildings in the UK.	Public	Materials (CLT)	https://www.architecture.com/StirlingPrize/Awards2015/SouthWestWessex/KeynshamCivicCentreandOneStopShop.aspx	
Eden Centre, Cornwall, UK	The Eden Centre incorporates biome architecture inspired by nature, context specific designs and low energy buildings to be one of the most iconic buildings in the world.	Public	Education	https://www.edenproject.com/eden-story/behind-the-scenes/architecture-at-eden	@edenproject
Brockholes Visitor Centre, Preston, UK	A sustainable building in the middle of a flood plain, the Visitor Village is built on a concrete pontoon floating on a lake and incorporates the highest environmental standards – BREEAM Outstanding.	Public	Materials	http://www.brockholes.org/green-statement	@visitBrockholes
Waste House, Brighton, UK	The Brighton Waste House investigates strategies for constructing a contemporary, low energy, permanent building using over 85% 'waste' material drawn from household and construction sites.	Housing	Waste	http://arts.brighton.ac.uk/business-and-community/the-house-that-kevin-built	@WasteHouse
WikiHouse, (online)	WikiHouse is an online construction kit helping people design and build beautiful, low-energy homes customised to their needs.	Housing	Materials	http://www.wikihouse.cc	@WikiHouse
Incredible Edible, Todmorden, Yorkshire, UK	Growing fruit, herbs and vegetables around Todmorden that are for everyone to share.	Community	Urban agriculture	https://www.incredible-edible-todmorden.co.uk/projects	@incredibledible
Bright Building Re:Centre, Bradford University, UK	Its function is to be a hub, where knowledge and experience – both practical and theoretical – are shared between all users of the centre and their associates. The building itself contains a wealth of fascinating operational features in its approach to energy, ergonomics, heating and airflow. BREEAM Outstanding.	Education	Circular economy, natural materials	http://www.bradford.ac.uk/recentre	@the_re_centre
Alliander HQ Duiven, Arnhem, NL	Transporting energy and gas to 3.3 million customers through their energy infrastructure, Alliander also facilitates an open energy market and supports sustainable energy choices. First renovation project in the Netherlands to obtain BREEAM-NL outstanding.	Commercial	Circular economy	https://www.alliander.com/en http://www.archdaily.com/777783/alliander-hq-rau-architects	

SOCIAL MEDIA SOURCES

You can follow, engage with and share FutuREstorative thoughts at @ FutuREstorative and #FutuREstorative.

Within Chapter 7 we explored how projects and organisations, even sustainability certification schemes, should adopt a net-positive approach to knowledge sharing, inspiring the next generation and future projects. Accessing all the knowledge shared can seem daunting. However there is no such thing as information overload, just poor information management.

Trust is Cheaper than Control

Having a robust and clear social media policy that describes what staff can do and cannot do is essential to ensure staff can be advocates for sustainability messages, stories and achievements. Policies typically consist of two parts: a) guidelines and b) how-to manual, and follow the P.O.S.T. structure of People (who), Objectives (why), Strategy (how) and Technology (what).

We should view social media feeds as a radio stream, constantly streaming programmes across countless stations and languages. We use our radio receiver to filter and tune in to the programmes we want to listen to. And so we should with social media, using lists, searches and aggregators to tune in to that which is important to us.

Following are the filters used by the author, along with curated 'influencer' lists of those active on social media worthy of following and adding to your personal information and knowledge feeds.

Twitter – Lists

An organisation may have just one sustainability or environmental guru to keep abreast of development, best practice and general sustainability buzz. Imagine if you had a global team. That's the beauty and power of linking to and engaging with fellow sustainability professionals, experts and advocates on Twitter. My (private) list of sustainability-related accounts is my first port of call to refresh sustainability thinking. It's like having your own team of experts on tap. While you can (and perhaps should) follow others, sustainability lists, developing your own, finely crafted list is a learning experience in itself.

SUGGESTED TWITTER LISTS	
FutuREstorative	https://twitter.com/fairsnape/lists/futurestorative
Living Future Thinkers	https://twitter.com/fairsnape/lists/living-future-thinkers
LBC Ambassadors – amazing volunteers who support the Living Building Challenge through the ILFI Ambassador Network	https://twitter.com/livingbuilding/lists/volunteer-ambassadors
Outdoors and wildness	https://twitter.com/fairsnape/lists/outdoors+wilderness
CSR Thought Leaders	https://twitter.com/fairsnape/lists/csr-thought-leaders

Flipboard

Google Reader used to be the author's go-to aggregator, replaced a number of years ago by Flipboard which provides an aggregated feed of sustainability sources from around the world; from mainstream media, twitter, online curated lists and more. Indispensable.

In addition to Twitter lists, the author's Flipboard stream also includes feeds from: Guardian Sustainability Business, Treehugger, 2degrees, CSRwire, Atlantic, all filtered to pick up built environment and/or sustainability threads.

Designing Buildings Wiki

An open wiki based forum that enables the sharing and finding of information across all disciplines of the built environment where 'Anyone can create articles about subjects they know and find articles on subjects they don't'.

Instapaper or Evernote

Platforms or 'apps' such as Instapaper and Evernote allow the curation of your own library of shared articles, blogs and papers that can be read later, off line.

SOCIAL MEDIA REFERENCES	
Flipboard	http://www.flipboard.com
Author's Flipboard 'magazines'	http://flip.it/TbeDH
Designing Buildings Wiki	http://www.designingbuildings.co.uk/wiki/Home
Instapaper	http://www.instapaper.com
Evernote	http://www.evernote.com

Social Media Influencer Lists

Social media influencer lists are sourced, curated and ranked from influence algorithms managed by organisations such as Klout and Kred. Klout[10], the more common, uses social media analytics to rank users with a score of 1 to 100, based on the engagement and interaction with content shared: the higher the score, the greater the breadth and strength of online social influence. Irrespective of the ranking, the lists provide a great who's who community around a particular theme.

SUGGESTED INFLUENCER LISTS	
Built Environment Top 500	http://sustmeme.com/top-500-leaderboards/built-environment-top-500
CSR and Responsible Business	https://www.rise.global/csr-business
Circular economy	http://sustmeme.com/top-500-leaderboards/circular-economy-top-500
BIM	http://sustmeme.com/top-500-leaderboards/bim-top-500

1   http://www.aldoleopold.org/AldoLeopold/leopold_bio.shtml
2   http://www.patagonia.com/us/patagonia.go?assetid=3351
3   https://discoverjohnmuir.com/
4   http://www.rachelcarson.org/
5   http://www.interfaceglobal.com/sustainability.aspx
6   http://www.paulhawken.com/paulhawken_frameset.html
7   http://www.monbiot.com/about/
8   https://open.spotify.com/user/mnbr/playlist/5rNf3WG6qgKOJ5CoqwTUk1
9   Case studies of Living Building Challenge projects can be found on the ILFI pages www.ilfi.org
10 https://www.klout.com

EPILOGUE
'IT'S JUST SUSTAINABILITY'

Throughout this book we have seen many innovations, many inspirations and many approaches that will help us make the transition towards a restorative sustainable future.

Yet none of this innovation, technology, biomimicry, biophilia or digital thinking will progress our sustainability performance if we do not have a matched and parallel improvement in equality, equity, diversity and justice.

And now, as we strive for a 1.5°C cap on global warming and the attendant carbon reduction, we need to ensure that equity and equality remain at the top of every sustainability agenda.

There can be no sustainability in an unequal world. Indeed sustainability should embrace the three E's of ecology, economy and equality.

As part of our sustainability journey, the language of construction also needs to evolve – from one that is perhaps too combative, technical and confrontational to one that is mindful, and embraces a language of collaboration, sharing, care and love. There are signs that the language of business is changing as it incorporates more diverse, open and inclusive approaches.

I am heartened by the interest in and pursuit of schemes such as BCorp and JUST recognition by built environment organisations, clients and manufacturers, yet such social responsibility recognitions really do need to become commonplace here in the UK.

I return to and close, for now, with one of the most important and powerful of the Living Building Challenge's aims: the transition to a socially just, ecologically restorative and culturally rich future.

INDEX

IMAGE CREDITS

Martin Brown

1, 9, 15, 17, 23, 25, 29, 33, 37,
49 (both), 65, 72, 75, 77, 79, 81,
83–85, 91, 93, 96 (both), 101,
108–110, 115, 118, 137, 145, 153

Carbon Visuals:
www.carbonvisuals.com

107

Conlon Construction

53

freeimages.com
Front cover, ii

IBE Partnerships
22 (both)

Nic Lehoux

88

UN: http://www.unmultimedia.
org/radio/english/wp-content/
uploads/2016/01/sdg-poster.jpg

50

University of Brighton

105